HOW TO BE AN
INCLUSIVE
LEADER

SECOND EDITION

HOW TO BE AN
INCLUSIVE
LEADER

Your Role in Creating Cultures of Belonging Where Everyone Can Thrive

JENNIFER BROWN

BK°

Berrett–Koehler Publishers, Inc.

Berrett-Koehler Publishers, Inc.
1333 Broadway, Suite 1000
Oakland, CA 94612-1921
Tel: (510) 817-2277
Fax: (510) 817-2278
www.bkconnection.com

ORDERING INFORMATION

Quantity sales. Special discounts are available on quantity purchases by corporations, associations, and others. For details, contact the "Special Sales Department" at the Berrett-Koehler address above.

Individual sales. Berrett-Koehler publications are available through most bookstores. They can also be ordered directly from Berrett-Koehler: Tel: (800) 929-2929; Fax: (802) 864-7626; www.bkconnection.com.

Orders for college textbook / course adoption use. Please contact Berrett-Koehler: Tel: (800) 929-2929; Fax: (802) 864-7626.

Distributed to the U.S. trade and internationally by Penguin Random House Publisher Services.

Berrett-Koehler and the BK logo are registered trademarks of Berrett-Koehler Publishers, Inc.

Printed in the United State of America.

Berrett-Koehler books are printed on long-lasting acid-free paper. When it is available, we choose paper that has been manufactured by environmentally responsible processes. These may include using trees grown in sustainable forests, incorporating recycled paper, minimizing chlorine in bleaching, or recycling the energy produced at the paper mill.

Library of Congress Cataloging-in-Publication Data

Names: Brown, Jennifer, 1971- author.
Title: How to be an inclusive leader : your role in creating cultures of
   belonging where everyone can thrive / Jennifer Brown.
Description: Second Edition. | Oakland, CA : Berrett-Koehler Publishers,
   [2022] | Revised edition of the author's How to be an inclusive leader,
   2019. | Includes bibliographical references and index.
Identifiers: LCCN 2022012432 (print) | LCCN 2022012433 (ebook) | ISBN
   9781523002009 (paperback) | ISBN 9781523002016 (pdf) | ISBN
   9781523002023 (epub) | ISBN 9781523002030
Subjects: LCSH: Leadership. | Personnel management. | Work environment.
Classification: LCC HD57.7 .B7656 2022 (print) | LCC HD57.7 (ebook) | DDC
   658.4/092—dc23/eng/20220311
LC record available at https://lccn.loc.gov/2022012432
LC ebook record available at https://lccn.loc.gov/2022012433

Second Edition

28 27 26 25 24 23 22   10 9 8 7 6 5 4 3 2 1

Book producer and text designer: Maureen Forys, Happenstance Type-O-Rama
Cover designer: Dan Tesser, Studio Carnelian

Several generations of very special women have served as my pilot lights.

To Deb Ziegler, who lifted me out of despair and showed me another way to make my voice matter.

To Mimi Brown with whom I've conspired for years on deep matters of the soul.

And most importantly, to my partner Michelle whose activist spirit and companionship I take respite in, every day of our lives together.

Contents

Preface

When I chose the title for the first edition of this book, *How to Be an Inclusive Leader*, including the word *how* was intentional. One of the questions I'm most often asked by leaders looking for guidance and direction is "How do I start?" Interestingly enough, for many leaders, it's figuring out the *how* that's holding them back.

What we expect of leaders has been upended, leaving many leaders unmoored and navigating through new, uncharted territory. In the past, we looked to our leaders for certainty and decisiveness. We expected them to lead with authority, to have all the answers. Now we expect our leaders to show humility, empathy, and vulnerability. We want them to willingly admit what they don't know. We ask them to be resilient in the face of criticism, to embrace and talk about their discomfort and mistakes.

The very essence of how leaders have understood their role and their responsibility to others—and to society—is being questioned and challenged. To add to it all, leaders are having to pivot through this uncertainty in the public eye. I wrote this book to equip those leaders who have ever felt uncertain about their next steps with a path forward.

In the first edition of the book, I introduced the Inclusive Leader Continuum to guide individuals through the very personal and emotional learning journey they undertake to become inclusive leaders—no matter where they are starting from. The four stages of the Continuum—Unaware, Aware, Active, and Advocate—formed the underpinnings of the first edition, and they do again in this new second edition. The first edition of the book proved to be a success, and I have had many opportunities to use the teachings in it as a construct in my consulting work, speaking engagements, and executive coaching. Through that work, I have been continually collecting new insights, listening to new stories, and discovering new tools. This is really what has led me to write the second edition of the book. There is that much more I want to share.

What started as minor revisions to the first edition kept growing in scope. I added a new chapter that delves deep into what holds many leaders back and the role identity and privilege play. I like to think of the chapter as a "call-in" to those leaders who are still on the sidelines. As leaders, we can bring so much to the change effort and we are already equipped to do this. I also developed Discussion Guides for each chapter to make the learning more actionable, and I added new stories that demonstrate so well what inclusive leadership actually looks like in practice.

I've had the good fortune to work with leaders who grasp the extent to which the playing field isn't level and understand they have a role in fixing that. They lead with purpose and get to work changing systems. But the reality is, many other leaders haven't yet awakened to the realities around them, and others might have awakened to those realities yet are still reluctant to get involved in the change effort. I hope this second edition will help leaders at any of these stages to get involved and step into their roles as diversity, equity, and inclusion (DEI) champions, advocates, and allies.

I am proud that the Inclusive Leader Continuum has enabled so many to ground themselves in their learning journey, to become true instruments of change. Solving for inequities and achieving meaningful change has elevated the importance of DEI and requires the personal commitment and involvement of all, especially those who have great access and influence. The need for inclusive leadership has never been more urgent. If we want a more just world, we need to grasp the urgency of our own role and responsibility because our role is necessary in the change equation.

No matter your title, or how advanced you already consider yourself to be as an inclusive leader, I believe this book will help you evolve and motivate you to take action. It's time to get comfortable being uncomfortable. It's time to activate your power and influence. It's time to roll up your sleeves and get off the sidelines. We need all hands on deck to make change happen.

I believe we all have the capacity to develop into the inclusive leaders the world, and the workplace, need. The time is now, so let's get started.

Introduction

Not everything that is faced can be changed, but nothing can be changed until it is faced.

—JAMES BALDWIN

There is a sea change underway. When I wrote the first edition of this book, organizations and their leaders were already navigating through a period of dramatic change. Globalization, population shifts, the climate crisis, advances in technology, political divides, and a range of other societal issues were spilling over into the workforce, creating new and unprecedented challenges for leaders. Since then, the rate of change has only accelerated.

The global pandemic made permanent dramatic shifts to the way that work is done. The murder of George Floyd in 2020 and the social movements that followed put a spotlight on the harsh reality that too many people in the United States continue to experience discrimination, racism, and violence. But it also served as a call to action, with millions of Americans marching, advocating, rallying, and organizing to put an end to centuries of systemic inequity.

The stakes for transformative conversations about diversity, equity, and inclusion (DEI) could not be higher. The wealth gap in the United States is the greatest it has ever been. Representation is still sorely lacking in boardrooms and at senior levels across every industry sector. Women and people of color are disproportionately overrepresented in low-skill, low-wage occupations, and disproportionately underrepresented in high-skill, high-wage jobs. Pay inequities, low wages, and lack of benefits continue to characterize many jobs in the nation's labor force. These are hard truths, and they have an impact on generations, communities, society, and the economy overall.

The growing transparency about inequities in the workplace has been a wakeup call for many organizations and leaders.

We're at a point in history in which people are finding their voices and using them to apply pressure on those organizations and leaders who are lagging behind social and demographic changes. The demand for equity is growing louder by the day. Today, employees expect companies to create value for all stakeholders—customers, communities, society—not just shareholders. Incoming generations of employees in particular crave purpose in their jobs. They are concerned with community, social responsibility, and the environment, and they look for a business purpose that aligns with those concerns. Customers are more discerning; they pay attention to business dealings, corporate ethics, how companies treat their people, and what they do for communities. If we want to resonate with the external consumer market as organizations, we must reflect those markets internally, both in our values and the representation in our workforce.

In this fast-changing world and marketplace, there really is no room for complacency. Our workplaces must evolve to center the individual and create cultures that accept, support, and respect differences and policies and practices that promote DEI.

In working with organizations and leaders during this period of massive transformation, I have found that the lessons of inclusive leadership are more relevant than ever. I originally revisited the first edition of the book with the goal of making the book more actionable and aligned with the shifts that need to happen in organizations in the current times. However, I found that once I started making updates, it was hard to stop. But I'm proud that the second edition of this book has evolved in ways that will help leaders and organizations respond to the changes unfolding around us in relevant, culturally competent ways and take action to address systemic inequities that persist in the workplace.

I believe we can and must do better. The inequity gaps we see today are a result of systemic failures that haven't been openly challenged and addressed. The root causes behind a lack of progress are almost always a lack of organizational understanding when it comes to what the issues are and a lack of courage on the part of senior leaders to take action and step into the role of advocate and activist on behalf of employees and the greater societal good.

As leaders, if we are ever to reach our full potential as employers and corporate citizens, we must consciously choose to take action. We must understand how inequities are manifested and exacerbated by institutions, workplaces, and social systems. We must uncover our prejudices and biases and take a hard look at ourselves and our participation in and perpetuation of inequitable systems.

Persisting Even When It's Challenging

Change is hard. I guarantee it is an uncomfortable and humbling journey to dive in and *really* understand how radically different many people's experience of the world is. Fear of the unknown—often about backlash and resistance—makes implementing change daunting, especially when we know little about the topics, are still learning the vocabulary, and sense we will be on the receiving end of criticisms and will be blamed personally for the inequities that are uncovered.

This is hard work—I know this personally. My early days as a DEI practitioner were driven from an activist mindset as a member of the LGBTQ+ community. I came out in my twenties at a time when you could still get fired in the workplace for being gay or experience harassment or violence if you walked down the street with the person you loved. Sadly, this is still the case in far too many parts of the world. The workplace was broken for me, and I used my voice as a community member to advocate for equity and inclusion. I led with a marginalized mindset and my identities as a woman and member of the LGBTQ+ community. I founded my company with this mindset and committed myself to the role of an advocate and to empowering other marginalized communities.

But as I've progressed through my own journey to become an inclusive leader, I've come to better understand the other identities I hold, those that enable me to function more easily in the world, that provide me with certain advantages that aren't available to many others. When I said earlier that it is a humbling and uncomfortable journey to become an inclusive leader, I meant it personally. When I began to learn more about how the privileged aspects of my identity afforded me access and platforms not available to many others, I felt guilt and shame and wasn't sure anymore where I fit in the change effort or what my role should be.

But that's the thing about identity. None of us is a monolith. Although I have experienced marginalization as a woman and member of the LGBTQ+ community, I also have positional power and social capital many others lack. I've realized that I share certain identities with many in senior leadership—I am White and cisgender, as well as a member of the generation that tends to dominate leadership ranks today. These elements provide me with some automatic trust and connection in what can be challenging conversations. Because of these shared aspects of identity, I am able to gain access, tap into networks, and leverage contacts to have my message heard at different levels, on different platforms. I realized these were tools I could also wield in the change effort.

> *As I've come to realize the potential—and impact—of all of my identities, my definition of doing enough has changed dramatically.*

It can be challenging to learn about your identity and grapple with issues related to privilege. It's a complex and loaded topic that can hold people back because they don't know what role they play in the change effort or how and if they should get involved. But leaders have a particularly important role in making change happen. To provide guidance and direction, I added a new chapter that delves deep into the role identity and privilege play in propelling change. I like to think of the chapter as a call-in to those leaders who are still on the sidelines.

My goal for this book is to help you grow your capacity to contribute to positive change and a more equitable and inclusive future. We can't outsource the work to others or delegate it to the diversity team or diversity leaders in our organizations. We *all* have a responsibility to act.

A New Type of Leadership Is Called For

Power and authority are changing fundamentally. Today's workplaces are full of outdated management practices and the very premises around which many leaders have built their careers, and perhaps organized their lives, are being challenged. We're in the midst of a chaotic and uncertain time in which the workplace is literally being reinvented and leaders are being asked to step up in new and different ways. A new type of leadership is called for. Marshall Goldsmith's book title *What Got You Here Won't Get You There* rings true here. It's time to throw out the playbook and correct course.

> *We're in the midst of a chaotic and uncertain time in which the workplace is literally being reinvented and leaders are being asked to step up in new and different ways.*

I believe that the mindset and skills needed to be an inclusive leader will be top of mind in nearly every organization as we move deeper into the twenty-first century and respond to the emerging challenges we face as organizations and leaders. Think of your inclusive leader journey as an investment in yourself and your career stock, no matter what your level in your organization. As a leader who deeply understands the challenges we face and the value of inclusion, you will have the right kind of skills to get the most out of your team and navigate through this time of great disruption. But I also anticipate and am confident that you will discover much more.

Inclusive leaders operate on a more personal level, building connections to people at all levels and from all identity groups, to better understand the problems at hand and what's needed to fix them. Those same qualities that were once seen as signs of weakness have now emerged as the key attributes of effective leadership. We value and expect leaders who are vulnerable, empathetic, purpose-driven and socially responsible and who are transparent about their journey.

Inclusive leaders are great leaders in the traditional sense, but they also lead with an additional vigilance, care, and intention. They deeply understand that the status quo only works for certain identity groups and that many people are having very different experiences in society and the workplace. They recognize where and when they can step in and use their voice to address inequities and they endeavor to tackle those inequities at the root. They understand their identities and biases and recognize how they have shaped the way they view the world and the people around them. They take a strong stand against bias and discrimination, even in their most subtle forms.

Inclusive leaders understand the capital they have access to, and they know how to deploy it for the greater good. Inclusive leaders are by nature dedicated to the thriving of others, particularly those who have struggled proportionally more to be heard and valued. They align themselves in solidarity with marginalized groups to amplify the voices and experiences of these groups, and they leverage their power and influence to accelerate the change they seek. Through their intentional and visible commitment to DEI, they are able to instill high levels of trust in their organizations, which in turn drives the followership that is needed to achieve real change. When senior leaders get involved and set clear expectations for equity and inclusion, it can send a ripple effect throughout the organization.

Inclusive leaders understand that the status quo only works for certain identity groups and that people are having radically different experiences in society and the workplace.

An important aspect of being an inclusive leader is understanding and internalizing the difference between *equality* and *equity*, yet I've observed that many leaders often use the terms interchangeably. Although the two terms seem similar, they mean distinctly different things, and the implementation of one versus the other can lead to dramatically different outcomes for marginalized people. In this second edition, I have intentionally prioritized the concept of equity and its role in the change effort. In reality, equity has become a core pillar of diversity and inclusion.

Equality assumes that each individual can succeed as long as they are given the same resources, fair treatment, and access to opportunities. In the workplace, equality looks like a one-size-fits-all approach to rules, policies, protocols, and opportunities for all employees. Although at first glance this may seem like a good inclusion strategy, companies often fail to acknowledge that not all employees are starting from the same place, or share the same set of experiences and circumstances, and that the journey is much harder for some people than others. By treating everyone the same, employee-specific needs are not taken into account.

Many of us were taught not to see or remark on differences. The statement "I don't see color" is an example of this. Instead of ignoring or denying differences, we need to acknowledge that we all have identities that impact our experience in the world and in the workplace. We need to recognize the impact of bias, stereotypes, and dominant cultures on people with marginalized identities, not have them swept under the rug by pretending they don't exist. When we recognize that the journey is more arduous for people of certain identities, we begin the real work of challenging systems and building equity.

Equity levels the playing field by recognizing that we don't all start from the same place or need the same things. Equity acknowledges that each employee has different needs and circumstances and ensures that each employee has the specific set of resources and opportunities that they need to succeed in the workplace. With a mindset toward equity, companies acknowledge specific needs related to demographics such as ethnicity, race, gender and gender identity, disabilities, and more. The needs and struggles faced by certain individuals are taken into account in decision-making and all employees have the support and resources they need to succeed.

Becoming an inclusive leader requires learning, reflection, and changing old habits and mindsets. But I believe that no matter whether you already consider yourself an advocate for diversifying the teams, communities, and workplaces in your life, or whether you are just starting to consider how some of the people around you might have a tougher climb up the ladder, this book will meet you where you are and help you progress to become a more inclusive leader.

A New Theory of Change: The Inclusive Leader Continuum

Over years of doing DEI work with countless organizations and leaders, I started noticing commonalities in leaders' perspectives and learning patterns. The people who were just beginning to understand the importance of inclusion had similar struggles and opportunities. Similarly, the people at the other end of the spectrum—those who had dedicated their careers to becoming advocates for those who are less represented (including themselves, in some cases) also had their own set of struggles and opportunities.

Because I had gotten to know so many people on their journey to becoming more inclusive leaders, it seemed natural to develop a multistage model for learners to use to identify their current state—in terms of knowledge and mindset—and most importantly, to anticipate next steps and develop goals for progress *toward* something. As human beings, we need to have at least a sense of what we're shooting for.

In the book, I use the Inclusive Leader Continuum as a four-stage framework to help individuals at all levels locate themselves and progress forward in their journeys to become inclusive leaders. I am so proud that the Continuum has enabled so many to ground themselves in their learning journeys and has given them a common structure and language to not only share about those journeys, but to get and give support to others along their way. This is not work we undertake alone.

The four stages of the Continuum are the same four stages in this second edition of the book as they were in the first. To make your journey more actionable, in this second edition, I have created a new structure for each of the stages, added new stories, and shared new tips. In addition, I have provided Discussion Guides for each of the four stages.

Here are the four stages:

UNAWARE   In the Unaware stage, you learn more about the experiences and challenges that people with other identities face. You educate yourself about the concept of bias and begin to examine your own biases and how they impact your perceptions of the world and the people around you. You embrace humility and acknowledge what you don't know.

AWARE   In the Aware stage, you learn more about the concept of privilege and understand better that the playing field is not level for everyone. You educate yourself about your own identities and those of other people and how our identities shape the way we experience the world around us. As you learn more about different lived experiences, you develop empathy and are motivated to contribute to the change effort.

ACTIVE   In the Active stage, you put your learning into action. You take risks in the interests of positive change and embrace a mindset of failing forward. You allow yourself to be vulnerable. You share your story and seek out the stories of other people. You lead and participate in difficult and uncomfortable conversations as learning opportunities. You dive deeper into DEI and get personally involved.

ADVOCATE In the Advocate stage, you leverage your power and influence to propel change. You draw attention to systemic inequities and get involved in solving them. You work in allyship with others to shift systems and behaviors and take action to disrupt the status quo. You exhibit resilience when you encounter resistance and continue to move forward even when it means breaking away from old norms and groups.

During this journey, it's essential that you don't become critical of yourself or others or place judgment based on where people are in the Continuum. Instead, the goal is to focus on making progress. Everyone who reads this book will be starting from a different place, and we all have a great deal to learn at every stage. That's why I recommend reading through each stage in this book no matter where you think your starting point might be.

It's also important to point out that the four stages of the Continuum are not presented as pejorative or value judgments, but rather neutrally, in a circular versus linear shape. The iterative nature of the model is important to me because there is so much to learn, and language and context are always evolving.

Sometimes we leap forward, and have great success, and sometimes we step back and regroup, recognizing how little we know.

We all reside somewhere among the four stages when it comes to our general mindset and daily actions, and there are no judgments about where you find yourself today. Some inclusive leaders bloom late in life into the desire to change and grow—maybe thanks to a single point in time, or an aha moment, or a series of realizations over time—while others grow up already more attuned to the world around them and the part they have to play. Whether your journey ignites with one moment or takes many years, the important thing is that you've started.

In addition to residing in one of these stages for our mindset, we revisit each of these stages over and over again when we learn about demographics and experiences that are new to us. For example, even though it's my job to know about DEI and I'm a woman and a member of the LGBTQ+ community, I don't begin to assume advocate-level knowledge of all unique groups of people in the world. So when I broaden my knowledge on, say, military veterans' unique challenges and opportunities when they reenter the civilian workforce, I start back at the beginning of the Continuum and make my way forward.

You will have the same experience with the Continuum. It's not a linear journey that we travel only once. We travel forward and backward many times as we learn, make mistakes, and grow. All of this is to be expected. It can help to think of your growth toward becoming an inclusive leader as a new habit and mindset you want to build. The good news is, there isn't a wrong starting point if your intent is to grow.

To get a sense of where you are at this moment, please consider pausing and taking our Inclusive Leader Assessment before you proceed; it will give you a starting point from which to begin to observe your own learning journey in action.

NOTE To support your learning journey and discover where you are currently on the Inclusive Leader Continuum, take our proprietary online assessment at inclusiveleaderthebook.com.

Call to Action

Our choices right now matter more than ever, for current and future generations. If we don't unpack and process how we are showing up at this moment in time, we will be unable to contribute in all the ways we are capable of—and in all the ways that are sorely needed, now more than ever. As change agents, we all have our best roles to play—our strongest cards. Each of us contains change tools, which include not just what we know, but who we are and how we appear. The question we must ask ourselves is "Am I effectively using everything I have been given to create informed positive change?"

We have much at stake in making our workplaces more equitable and inclusive. We have the opportunity to build a different future, a better future. All of us are needed—to chip in, to contribute, to get involved—not just on paper, registering our good intentions, but doing the actual work of change, especially *within* ourselves, and following a learning path with discipline and commitment.

So I invite and urge you to learn with humility, connect with empathy, share with vulnerability, and lead with courage and resilience. I believe that we each have the *capacity* to effect change, especially if we've been waiting on the sidelines. Our sphere of influence is bigger than we perceive, and we leave much on the table every day when we don't see our role in driving change. Let's collectively commit to building a more equitable future together.

The Inclusive Leader Continuum

ONGOING RE-EVALUATION

PHASE TWO
Aware

PHASE THREE
Active

PHASE ONE
Unaware

Inclusive Leader Continuum

PHASE FOUR
Advocate

2 · 3 · 1 · 4

UNAWARE
You think diversity is compliance-related and simply tolerate it. It's someone else's job—not yours.

AWARE
You are aware that you have a role to play and are educating yourself about how best to move forward.

ACTIVE
You have shifted your priorities and are finding your voice as you begin to take meaningful action in support of others.

ADVOCATE
You are proactively and consistently confronting inequities and discrimination and working to bring about change in order to prevent it on a systemic level.

Private // Low Risk // Individual Perspective ⟩⟩ Public // High Risk // Organizational Perspective

To support your learning journey and discover where you are currently on the Inclusive Leader Continuum, take our proprietary online assessment at inclusiveleaderthebook.com.

CHAPTER ONE

Finding Your Role as an Inclusive Leader

Every society has its protectors of status quo and its fraternities of the indifferent who are notorious for sleeping through revolutions. Today, our very survival depends on our ability to stay awake, to adjust to new ideas, to remain vigilant and to face the challenge of change.

—MARTIN LUTHER KING JR.

Over the past several decades, companies have invested heavily in DEI programs and initiatives. Yet most programs that exist today are still focused on compliance and performative actions, are siloed in HR departments, and lack the commitment and involvement of senior leaders. Few are designed to shift systems or address the patterns of exclusion, oppression, and disadvantage underrepresented and marginalized groups continue to face in the workplace.

To build a more inclusive and equitable future, leaders in positions of power and influence must play an active role in disrupting the status quo. The hard truth is that, with a labor market that's becoming more competitive and more diverse, leaders who aren't making an effort to become more inclusive, accountable, and equity minded will be left behind. Yet I have found that most leaders are still holding back.

In my twenty years of DEI work, I often encounter three types of leaders. I have worked with some leaders who really get it, who grasp the extent to which the playing field is not equal, and who understand that they have a role in fixing that. They lead with purpose and are on the front lines of challenging inequities and changing systems. When we work with leaders like this, we can dig in and get right to work.

Then there are other leaders who have awakened to the realities of the world around them but are reluctant to get involved. Many don't do anything because they're afraid of making a mistake, of getting it wrong. This is new territory, and they don't feel like they have the right words or vocabulary to step into the conversation. They are not even sure if they are welcome. So they stay on the sidelines and their lack of action maintains and protects the status quo.

And there are still too many leaders who just don't understand the depth and impact of the inequities that surround them. They don't see what any of it has to do with them. With these leaders, I can't count how many times deflections fill the room when I start to talk about DEI and why it matters. These are just a few that are verbalized:

- People need to stop being so sensitive.

- I'm buried—I don't have time to prioritize this work.

- I prefer to see past race and gender—we're all just people.

- We did unconscious bias training, so I don't think we have any major issues here.

- Are you suggesting we should have quotas?

I think of these as deflections because they aren't genuine curiosities about the way forward; they are barriers and distractions that are often raised to obscure or delay responsible action. But being unwilling to look clear-eyed at the dramatic changes around us—in our colleagues, in our professional landscape, in global markets—is a classic tactic of avoidance.

Don't get me wrong—I don't think of these types of leaders as bad people. But I *do* think many people who are in leadership roles probably have no idea what many of their colleagues are going through at work since the experience is likely vastly different from their own reality. And because they don't understand the problems people with other identities experience, they aren't able to take the brave and necessary leadership actions needed.

When the world around us looks like us and is designed to work for us, it can be hard to grasp the extent to which the playing field is skewed in our favor. For those who have more privileged backgrounds, it can be easy to dismiss or downplay the experiences and outcomes of people who've been historically marginalized and underrepresented in a given system. The truth is, privilege can be invisible to those of us who have it.

The reality is that biases and inequities have permeated just about every aspect of the professional world, from decades (if not centuries) of pattern build-up. This is not a problem that will just go away if we all think good thoughts or avoid facing the truth about the systems around us. As the ground rapidly shifts under our feet, our inability to see the once-in-a-generation opportunity for change is a liability for all of us. Our future impact—and legacy—depend on how we step up during this moment.

*Our inability to see this
once-in-a-generation opportunity
for change is a liability for
all of us.*

The unwillingness to look at what needs to change and how we as leaders can contribute is a missed opportunity to evolve, to transform, and to equip ourselves to build something that works for more of us—and that will benefit *all* of us.

Unfortunately, no business strategy, including DEI, will deliver optimal results if individuals with power and influence are disconnected from that strategy. If the very people who are in the position to make change happen are unaware there's a problem, in denial that inequities exist, or throwing their hands up about the supposed complexity—or cost—of fixing the problem, we will never scratch the surface of what's possible.

> *The arc of the moral universe is long, but it bends towards justice.*
>
> —MARTIN LUTHER KING JR.

I have always found this quote by MLK inspirational. In the midst of confusion, overwhelm, and uncertainty about our increasingly chaotic world, it gives me hope that an inevitable shift toward a more just world is possible, where all people are treated equitably and respectfully. But most of all, I don't believe his words condone passivity or inaction, for any of us.

It used to be enough for me to take solace in MLK's words, but because I've been focused on building more inclusive workplaces now for nearly two decades, I've come to realize a hard fact: just a relative few of us are doing the lion's share of the work to bend the arc.

The pressing question this leaves us with is, who's missing from the change team, and why?

Historically, DEI programs have been centered around the needs of marginalized and underrepresented employees and addressing the barriers and inequities these groups experience. Although unintended, the impact of this focus has distanced many people in leadership positions from understanding their potential contribution and role in DEI efforts.

For the most part, it is members of marginalized communities who take up the mantle to do the work of challenging discriminatory practices and systems. But every time we automatically turn to the woman, the Black or Brown leader, the person with a disability, or any other individual belonging to a marginalized community to take responsibility for identifying and addressing organizational inequities, we are abdicating our own role and responsibility. This needs to change.

Each of us must begin to take responsibility for the roles that we can play, especially if we hold positions of privilege, power, and influence but have been passive or inactive. We may not have been directly affected by inequities; we might feel it's not our fight. But this in itself is a privilege: to have the choice to remain on the sidelines in the fight for equity while others struggle.

The ability and choice to remain
on the sidelines is a privilege
available to some—not all.

Whenever my company begins work on an organization's DEI strategy, we recommend involving top leaders. When it comes to disrupting the status quo and creating equity in the workplace, much power lies with leaders who set the standards and tone for everything from who gets hired and who advances to what the workplace culture looks like. We understand that without their buy-in and personal involvement, our efforts will have more limited impact and will be more difficult to sustain. The reality is, leaders are an influential employee group in the workforce to drive real change.

As leaders, we can't sit back and wait for the arc of history to bend by itself or keep expecting others to put their shoulders to the wheel. If we want a more just world, one in which the playing field begins to equalize, we need to grasp the urgency of our own role and responsibility to bend the arc. We have to do our part, and we still have a long way to go.

Finding Your Way into the Conversation

Privilege is not in and of itself bad; what matters is what we do with privilege. We have to share our resources and take direction about how to use our privilege in ways that empower those who lack it.
—AUTHOR AND ACTIVIST GLORIA JEAN WATKINS (PEN NAME BELL HOOKS)

The greatest opportunity of inclusive leadership is being able to interrogate ourselves about the role we play in the systems around us and how we can affect positive change in those systems. Yet, when it comes to addressing systemic inequities, it is almost always a lack of understanding on the part of leaders about what the issues are, what role they should play in resolving those issues, and how they get started that is holding them back.

One way to get started is to do your homework to learn more about the privilege you hold and to understand better how your privileges may contribute—even unintentionally—to discrimination, inequity, and exclusion. As you learn more about your privileges, you will come to recognize what parts of your world, your workplaces, and your communities work *for you* and are, indeed, optimized for you. You develop an awareness that the same system can be experienced completely differently by different people. The fundamental question about privilege is this: *How much of my world was built with me in mind?*

During the COVID-19 pandemic, we saw the answers to that question play out before us. Asian communities were "othered" during the pandemic and scapegoated for the virus merely because they looked like the people from the part of the world where it was first reported. Hate crimes against the community increased significantly throughout the pandemic across the world. But the Asian American community has always experienced inequities, exclusion, violence, and dehumanization. Historically, anti-Asian racism predictably increased during times of war, economic declines, and disease. These are hard truths.

As the pandemic wore on, Black and Hispanic communities were hit the hardest. They were overrepresented in low-paying jobs that were less likely to provide health coverage or paid time off. They got sick and died at higher rates. They disproportionately held front line jobs with high levels of public contact that put them at greater risk of contracting the virus while others with more privileged identities had the opportunity to safely shelter in place. These types of disparities didn't happen overnight in the face of a pandemic. They have always been with us and are deeply embedded in systems and structures around us.

The pandemic was also devastating for women, with caregiving demands driving millions from their jobs. Yet women were paying a price for caregiving even before the pandemic. The advancement of women has always been hampered by workplace policies that fail to support work-life balance; the pandemic merely brought into focus the disproportionate burden women carry when it comes to caregiving and the cost of that burden to their careers. Despite the overwhelming evidence and research about the impact of caregiving on women, most companies continue to fail to prioritize their needs.

*As the pandemic made
so very clear, we may all weather
the same storm, but we are
in very different boats.*

Privilege is a fundamentally loaded topic, and for those of us with privileged identities, it can be difficult to talk about. In working with senior leaders over the years, I have noticed that many of them are uncomfortable with the concept of privilege, don't know how to deploy their privileges for systems change, or are ashamed of the personal advantages that privilege offers them.

Many of us assume that by admitting our privileges, we somehow invalidate how hard we have worked. We may assume that the label *privileged* implies we don't deserve to have what we have, or it infers that we have never experienced hardship. Having privilege does not mean that an individual is immune to life's hardships. But it does mean having an unearned benefit or advantage by nature of one's identity.

I have struggled with the concept of privilege personally. In many ways, people view me as the kind of person unlikely to experience any challenges with inequity. After all, I am White, cisgender, and able-bodied. I have other invisible privileges: I grew up in a safe home where I didn't want for anything and where I was told I could be anything I wanted. I had access to a quality education and the opportunity to go to the college of my choice. These aspects of my identity have enabled me to function more easily in the world, more safely, with more automatic—and often unearned—protections. They are the invisible, silent tailwinds that speed me along just that much more quickly.

I have also come to understand that my privilege is about what I did *not* have to experience, the ways in which I don't struggle on a daily basis—the ways in which I'm safer, more protected, more shielded from the harsh realities of bias, exclusion, and violence.

> *Privilege is also the way*
> *in which we didn't—and*
> *don't—have to struggle.*

Yet, for most of my adult life, I have also identified with and led from a mindset of marginalization as a member of the LGBTQ+ community and as a woman, each of which can be detrimental in the business world. I came out when I was twenty-two and struggled to find examples of professionals who were like me in the roles I aspired to fill one day. Very few women, and even fewer openly gay professionals, seemed to be at the top. Unfortunately, this is still the case.

Anxiety about my identities in the workplace often dominated my thoughts. I had a pervasive fear that if people knew the real me, it would hurt my relationships and my reputation. So, for a long time, I hid the parts of me that I feared would be rejected. I avoided sharing personal stories. I felt like an outsider at work.

As someone with a foot in several worlds of identity-based privileges as well as identity-based disadvantages, for decades I have been on my own journey of endeavoring to feel seen, heard, and valued, while at the same time grappling with how I can use my privilege and influence to drive equity and inclusion for others.

Privilege is not an absolute. It can coexist alongside identities that leave us feeling marginalized and disadvantaged.

Rather than feeling confused, frozen, or disconnected from the fight for equity, or ashamed of my place of privilege in many systems, I realized it's more important to understand what I *can* do, to learn more about the role I *can* play. For those of us who routinely benefit from privilege, the challenges are to acknowledge its existence, to make it visible to ourselves, and to leverage the advantages it confers.

I believe it is time to reframe the concept of privilege in a way that doesn't cause defensiveness, or fear, or keep us frozen in place but rather feels like something we can acknowledge, own, and activate.

All too often, I've observed that the concept of privilege is employed to *call out* or otherwise criticize and dismiss the potential contributions of people with privileged identities. I believe this is holding us back. Although it is critical for people belonging to dominant groups to understand the advantages their identities confer—and how people with other identities aren't afforded those same advantages—if we are only calling them out for being part of the problem, we are alienating them from getting involved in solving those same problems.

I'm not discouraging anyone from calling out individual harmful behaviors and microaggressions, but when we call out and dismiss entire groups of people only because of their privileged identities, we may inadvertently be distancing them from getting involved and using their power and influence for the greater good.

I encourage each of us to practice *calling in* behavior to invite people of all identities, including those with privileged identities, to take a seat at the table. Calling in creates the space for individuals to take responsibility, to learn more, and to do better. We will never build momentum to create meaningful change if we continue to work in isolation or as adversaries. We need to learn how to work in partnership and in solidarity.

Getting Off the Sidelines

Change will not come if we wait for some other person or if we wait for some other time. We are the ones we've been waiting for. We are the change that we seek.

—FORMER PRESIDENT OBAMA

There is no such thing as the perfect time or the right way to do this work. The time is now, and these conversations are already underway. It's incumbent on those of us whose identities make us insiders in a system to go first. The only choice we have is to step up and show up, however imperfectly—to get comfortable with being uncomfortable. If you aren't pushing yourself to do more and pushing others around you to improve too, chances are, you aren't really leading.

Being an inclusive leader starts with a spark to do better. That spark lives inside all of us, almost like a pilot light. It's always there, ready and waiting to create a bigger flame. Inclusive leaders have that spark. They have a genuine desire to make the world a better place. They are aware of, and know how to utilize, their power and privilege to raise issues, to challenge norms and behaviors, and to root out and prioritize core issues that perpetuate exclusionary dynamics. They push themselves as much as they push others.

When you have that spark, you start to see all the opportunities to better support others unfold. You want to *do* more. To learn, to grow, and to contribute. To challenge the status quo and participate in creating lasting change. To fulfill your potential as a person and as a leader. To leave things better than you found them.

The hardest part about becoming an inclusive leader can be that initial work to switch the pilot light on, to become aware that you are already equipped with the ability to make a difference, and to learn how much your efforts are needed.

But to ignite that light, you must uncover your biases and learn to manage them. You must own your privileges and the advantages they have afforded you and acknowledge that it is not an equal playing field for many around you. This can be an uncomfortable and humbling journey of self-discovery that's not always easy.

*Leadership is not leadership
unless it's uncomfortable.*

I deeply believe that each of us has the capacity to affect meaningful change. The question is, can you ignite your *will* to change?

This book lays out a step-by-step process to becoming a more inclusive leader, to finding your role and voice in affecting societal and workplace change. By deciding to read this book, you have demonstrated that you are already committed to growth, to pushing yourself, to being uncomfortable with your own limitations and inadequacies, and to opening yourself to the identities and experiences of others.

The road of inclusive leadership is a very personal one. As you dive into the four stages of the Inclusive Leader Continuum, I urge you to push yourself. To examine not only your own actions but also the ways that your inaction can create a safe space for broken systems to continue unchecked.

As leaders, our sphere of influence is bigger than we perceive, and we squander the resources we have access to every day we remain inactive and uninvolved. So, let's get started.

Chapter Discussion Guide

What You Can Do

- Learn more about the concept of privilege and how it personally advantages and disadvantages you and how that may be different for other groups of people.

- When thinking about the privileges you hold, what emotions come up for you? Why do you think that is? Are these emotions holding you back from activating your power and influence in the change effort?

- If you haven't gotten involved in your organization's DEI efforts, reflect on what's holding you back and start to think about what role you can play.

Conversation Starters

- Discuss the concept of privilege as a group, and explore how we all have identities that may advantage and disadvantage us to gain a better understanding of the unique lens with which we all view the world.

- Discuss as a group the different ways privilege plays out in your organization and workplace. Talk about how privilege benefits some and disadvantages others.

- Strategize ways the group can get more proactively involved in DEI and the change effort. Identify areas where you may need support, training, or education to approach this work in a meaningful and relevant way.

CHAPTER TWO

Unaware

In this stage, you learn more about the experiences and challenges that people with other identities face. You educate yourself about the concept of bias and begin to examine your own biases and how they impact your perceptions of the world and the people around you. You embrace humility and acknowledge what you don't know.

The moment when Microsoft's CEO, Satya Nadella, took the stage at the Grace Hopper Conference will always epitomize the Unaware stage for me. But it also signifies the opportunity we all have to learn with humility and grow from mistakes.

The year was 2014, and Nadella was in his first year as CEO. When asked for his advice regarding women's careers, and specifically about asking for raises, Nadella told the crowd of mostly women "It's not really about asking for the raise, but knowing and having faith that the system will actually give you the right raises as you go along. That's good karma. It will come back." He added, "That's the kind of person that I want to trust, that I want to give more responsibility to."[1]

Women reacted, online around the world, with shock, anger, and dismay. How could someone so powerful and with such a platform completely miss the reality of pay inequality—and even worse—claim that a system permeated with unexamined bias would actually do right by them in the end if they just waited long enough?

The experience at the Grace Hopper Conference awakened Nadella to the fact that organizations work better for some than others and that people struggle for a fair shake in ways he didn't know about. He reflected on his comments in later years, sharing that it was a "humbling learning experience." He explained that the advice he gave that day was advice he had received and followed in his own career and that he had underestimated the bias and inequities women experience in the workplace. He hadn't experienced this personally, and at that stage in his leadership evolution, he hadn't made a point to learn about it. In other words, he didn't know what he didn't know.

The journey to become an inclusive leader is a personal and imperfect one; we are bound to make mistakes along the way. But experiences like Nadella's can also be transformative when we embrace them as opportunities for growth and learning; they can help us shift the way we see the world and the people around us. This really is the invitation of the Unaware stage—to get the growth and learning started.

Since the Grace Hopper Conference, Nadella has been in many other headlines that applaud and recognize him for his work as an inclusive leader driving real change.[2] He has publicly shared how seeing the world through the eyes of his son with a disability has expanded his empathy and provided him with insight into the journeys of people with disabilities—how they interact with technology, and how technology can be made more accessible for them.

Since Nadella took the helm as CEO of Microsoft, he has leveraged his power and influence to prioritize accessibility and to change the way products are designed and developed and how people are recruited and hired at the company. So, in many ways, Nadella also exemplifies what inclusive leadership looks like in the Advocate stage.

It's important to remember that the Inclusive Leader Continuum is an ongoing, nonlinear process. Nadella's experience is a great example of how individuals can move back and forth between the different stages of the Continuum in their journey to become inclusive leaders.

Hallmarks of the Unaware Stage

In the Unaware stage, you revisit the history you were taught to better understand what may have been missing. You deepen your knowledge and understanding of the legacies of discrimination and the systemic inequities that persist today. You reach out to people from other identity groups to learn more about their lived experiences and how they differ from your own.

In this stage, you recognize that self-reflection and humility are critical to the process of becoming an inclusive leader. The reality is, if you haven't been directly affected by discrimination or inequities, it can be easy to misunderstand or tune out the problems and challenges other people face. In this stage, you develop awareness of what you don't know and accept with humility that you have a lot to learn.

During this stage you also dive deeper into learning more about the concept of bias. You examine your own biases and reflect on how they show up in your own beliefs and behaviors, how they influence your perceptions of the world and the people around you. You begin to recognize that workplace policies, practices, and systems also promote and perpetuate biases and inequities.

As you progress through this stage, it's common to feel uncomfortable and to find yourself becoming guilty, angry, or defensive. But you begin to recognize that discomfort is a sign of growth. You persist despite your discomfort and understand your involvement in the change effort is critical, especially if you are a leader.

Embracing and Practicing Humility

It is unwise to be too sure of one's own wisdom. It is healthy to be reminded that the strongest might weaken and the wisest might err.

—MAHATMA GANDHI

Learning with humility means we recognize that we don't know everything. I am reminded of this often, in big and small ways. Just recently, on a virtual panel, I used the word *paralyzed* to describe the way leaders can become frozen by the fear of saying or doing the wrong thing. Another panel member gave me feedback in the moment, reminding me that many people actually do experience paralysis, and we can choose alternative words to describe such mindsets that are more respectful of those people. I thanked her, and I now carry this learning forward with me and share it with others.

This is the practice of humility: a willingness to accept new ideas, information, and perspectives—even if they contradict our own views or expose our imperfections and those times we miss the mark. Humility reminds us that we don't know, understand, or have all the answers, and that we need to seek clarity and facts without the knee-jerk reaction so many of us have to agree or disagree. It means learning to check our egos at the door.

Wade Davis, a former NFL football player who later became the league's first LGBTQ+ inclusion consultant, once said that the compulsive need to be right is one of the biggest obstacles to building inclusion, particularly for the men he works with. That's why he begins every training with this question: Can you agree for today to be uninterested in being right?[3]

In agreeing to his request, participants actually feel a sense of relief from not having to know everything. Instead, Wade's request gives them permission to be present and to stay open to what they don't know. Wade's second question introduces another key way to help people focus on personal growth: For today, can you be uninterested in thinking of yourself as a good person?

When we give up the need to be right and instead become curious about what we don't know, suspending judgment as we educate ourselves about the reality of other people's circumstances and experiences, we have the opportunity to really learn—to challenge our past thinking and patterns and release their grip on the way we view the world.

In this context, the measure of leadership is not always having a perfect performance but showing up with humility and being willing to make mistakes and learn.

*Let's not make perfect
the enemy of the good.*

Educating Yourself and Learning More

Alternative facts have always been with us, and they've often been used to cover up some hard truths about our nation's history. In this stage, I encourage you to get out of your comfort zone and really push yourself to deepen your knowledge and understanding of topics including colonization, slavery, sexism, homophobia, xenophobia, and the legacies of discrimination and systemic inequity that persist today as a result.

For many of us, this means revisiting the history we were taught to better understand what may have been missing. Doing this is enriching and powerful, but it can also trigger defensiveness, anger, shame, and guilt. I personally have experienced many of these feelings as I've grappled with all that I didn't know and hadn't been exposed to or understood in our nation's history.

You can also reach out to people with other identity backgrounds to learn more about their lived experiences and how they may differ from your own. I have found that personal growth and change often start with an open dialogue—one that is not accusatory or emotionally charged but that is focused on a constructive perspective—one that asks: What can I learn from people whose experiences are different from my own?

Getting to know people on a personal level helps you see them as individuals rather than as stereotypes. Broaden your horizons. Branch out and connect with more coworkers who look different from you. Make an effort to make small talk and be more social with people outside of your regular circle. Attend a meeting or event that exposes you to members of different communities. Ask questions that get other people to open up. Open up yourself.

Sometimes a single conversation about divisive issues or a person's painful experience of inequity or exclusion can provide that aha moment in which you become aware that other people experience challenges and struggles you haven't experienced firsthand. But it's important that you remember to do your homework to understand the issues first, before you ask someone from a marginalized identity to make an effort to support your learning.

Before you ask others to educate you, make sure you've done your own homework to educate yourself.

If your organization has employee resource groups (ERGs), this is a good place to start. ERGs often have a wealth of information about the challenges marginalized and underrepresented communities face, both in society and in the workplace. Learn more about the ERGs in your organization and the issues they are addressing. But again, remember it is not ERG members' responsibility to educate or guide you through your learning journey.

I also urge you to reflect on the choices you make when picking a book to read, a movie to watch, or a social media account to follow. Do you seek perspectives that are different from your own when you make these choices?

Many of us live in echo chambers, continually seeking out the same perspectives over and over again. Echo chambers reinforce existing biases and beliefs and limit our exposure to new information and different perspectives. To avoid this, make a deliberate choice to consume different media; choose podcasts, TV shows, books, and movies where the creators and the people involved have different identities than you do.

In the Unaware stage, I encourage you to be curious about those lives and experiences that are different from your own and commit to getting out of your echo chambers. An important quality of an inclusive leader is having a growth mindset and being open to new information and perspectives.

Uncovering Bias

Some of the biggest obstacles that get in the way of inclusive leadership are the biases we hold—the cultural and social stereotypes, attitudes, opinions, and stigma we attach to certain groups of people.

We can be biased about just about anything—not just gender, skin color, or age, but also things like communication style, relationship status, political beliefs, or even what someone does in their free time. We see biases play out in society every day, impacting things like who gets invited to high stakes meetings, who is followed in a retail store, who gets pulled over by the police, or who gets blamed for a pandemic. These types of biased judgments cause us to make decisions that are neither rational nor fair.

If you're human, you're biased. We all have biases; they are the sum total of our socialization and life experiences—they are part of the lens through which we see the world. We were raised with the biases and belief systems of our parents and our communities, and they become deeply woven into our psyches. They show up in the quick and often inaccurate judgments we make based on limited facts and our personal life experiences. Think of them too as shortcuts that we use, to make sense of the massive amount of information we absorb every day. No matter how hard we try, they will pop up, over and over again, as they are deeply embedded and conditioned in us from a young age.

All of us have unconscious bias, meaning we have little to no awareness of our biases, and we may not even be aware we are thinking or acting in a biased way. Unconscious bias can show up in everyday interactions—who we choose to have lunch with (and what restaurant we decide to go to), who we decide to mentor, who we share business insights with, whose input we value, and so on. Unconscious bias also shows up as commonplace everyday slights, whether intentional or unintentional, that communicate negative attitudes or perceptions toward certain groups. These are often experienced as microaggressions. Unconscious bias impedes our ability to see the full person beyond the stereotypes and social narratives we subconsciously assign people with certain identities.

In working with clients, I have witnessed unconscious bias many times. For example, some male leaders unconsciously believe that women don't work as hard as men, or they don't put in the same hours as men, because they have more family-related responsibilities.

When a leader who holds this belief notices a gender wage gap in the workplace, he might think the gap is justified because he believes women are responding to competing demands. Instead of considering other causes of the gender wage gap, his biases support his belief that women aren't as committed to their jobs and therefore deserve less pay.

Another common type of bias I frequently see play out in the workplace is affinity bias. This continually plays out in our tendency to favor people who are like us in some way, when we automatically gravitate toward and trust those people who look like us or share some of our life experiences. A good example of this playing out in the workplace is when a person is hired because they share the same alma mater as the hiring manager.

This may seem like a micro-level example of affinity bias, but I believe it has a macro-level impact. A crisis of conformity still plagues C-suites and boardrooms across the world. In 2020, approximately 86 percent of Fortune 500 CEOs were White men, yet White men make up just 35 percent of the US population.[4] A landmark 2015 *New York Times* article reported that "fewer large companies are run by women than by men named John."[5] These examples show how bias can be so deeply entrenched in our thinking and beliefs that it can prevent other identity groups from finding a seat at the table.

> *Bias can be so deeply entrenched that it can prevent other identity groups from finding a seat at the table.*

Another form of bias I often see people struggle with is confirmation bias. We have a tendency to pay more attention to the information and views that uphold our beliefs and ignore information and views that challenge or contradict them.

For instance, if a White male leader believes that there aren't inequities in his organization and he only seeks the perspectives of other White leaders in the organization, their perspectives will likely reinforce his already existing belief that inequities don't exist. But if he asked leaders and employees of color about whether there are inequities in the workplace, he will likely get completely different perspectives. Unfortunately, this type of bias can prevent us from looking at situations objectively and understanding the complete picture.

Although I've only discussed three types of bias, it's important to note that there are multiple types of bias, and that it's incumbent on all of us to learn more about them and how they shape our perceptions, beliefs, and behaviors.

As inclusive leaders, your biases are some of the first things that need unpacking and a critical look. Spend some time reflecting on the following questions:

- What happens when you encounter someone new? Do you conclude specific information from your overall impression? Think critically about whether your initial conclusions are warranted. Stop yourself from making assumptions about others and their work, family life, interests, expertise level, background, speech, and so on.

- Think about the people you feel comfortable with and regularly seek out. Are you only engaging with people who look like you, who share your worldview? What is the reason behind your comfort level with these individuals?

- Now think of the people you connect with less frequently. People you don't seek out. Why is that? What stands in the way of forging better connections with these people?

It can be profound when you realize that you are biased and when you begin to recognize that workplace policies, practices, and systems also promote and perpetuate biases. It's important to understand that our workplaces were not built *by* or *for* all kinds of identities, but rather for those who originally built the modern workplace and still dominate its leadership ranks.

> *The reality is, most workplaces are biased toward what actually works for just a narrow group of architects.*

At this point in the Continuum, the goal is not to eliminate bias, which is in fact neurobiologically impossible, but to generate awareness. You *can* learn to mitigate for bias. Once you understand that we all are biased, you have the cognitive ability to self-correct. It's in your power to recognize when your biases and your behaviors are hurting, erasing, or impeding others. And this also means challenging bias when you see it in others and recognizing that when you don't speak up, you're enabling biased behavior to continue to cause harm.

This new awareness, and then the ability to choose different behaviors or actions, is the measure of inclusive leadership and something you will practice and get better at as you move through the Continuum. Unpacking our personal biases and checking bias in the systems around us informs much of the work ahead, and for many of us, will be a constant but necessary struggle. But becoming aware of biases is the first step toward solving them.

If you haven't already, I encourage you to take the Harvard Implicit Bias Test to deepen your awareness of your own biases and how they shape your view of the world.[6] Although it is not a perfect test, it is likely to provide you with insight to better understand the biases you have and to begin to question the ways they shape your decisions and behaviors.

Questioning Our Biases

As we dive deeper into the inclusive leader journey, we must build the capacity to continually check ourselves for ingrained biases and stereotypes we may hold about people with identities different than our own. One of the best ways to challenge ourselves is by increasing our proximity to difference, in the form of the people we surround ourselves with, as well as the frequency with which we interact across different identities.

I'm sharing a tool I've adapted called the Inner Circle Inventory, inspired by Amy Waninger in her book *Networking Beyond Bias*.[7] It's a powerful method to assess how bias influences the relationships we choose. The inventory will help you make a regular habit of examining who constitutes your inner circle. We all have our go-to people—they may be coworkers, friends, those we mentor, as well as those who mentor us. It might be easiest to think of this list as those we trust and feel most comfortable with, or those we talk to the most frequently, whether the setting is work or not.

The simple exercise of inventorying this circle to identify dimensions *different from ours* forces us to look for patterns in our relationships and better understand our tendency to seek comfort in sameness, and our discomfort with, and avoidance of, the unknown and the unfamiliar.

Follow the example in Figure 1. Write down the names of your trusted inner circle in the first column of a grid. Next, fill in the top row with various diversity dimensions (e.g., ethnicity, age, gender identity and expression, sexual orientation, education, disabilities, parenting status, political beliefs, socioeconomic background, etc.) Then, place an X for each person where their identity differs from your own in any given category. You can even total up the X marks to get a birds-eye view of where there is a lack of representation, of difference, in your life. Moving out of the Unaware stage means beginning to notice this kind of homogeneity and questioning how and why your exposure is so limited.

INITIALS OR FIRST NAME (NO FAMILY MEMBERS)	DIVERSITY DIMENSIONS					
	ETHNICITY	SEXUALITY	GENDER	ABILITY	ETC.	TOTAL Xs
Person 1	X		X	X		3
Person 2	X	X	X			3
Person 3			X			1
Person 4		X				1
Person 5	X	X	X			3
Person 6	X			X		2
Person 7			X			1
Person 8		X				1
Etc.						
Total Xs	4	4	5	2		15

Figure 1. Inner Circle Inventory

For some of us, and in some contexts, it's common to see our identities reflected around us—perhaps not at work, but in our friend groups, or vice versa. Many of us seek comfort in sameness, in shared identities and experiences; this is a key part of human need. The inclusive leadership journey's foundation, however, is to proactively challenge our usual choices—the easy choices—and to regularly push ourselves to seek more and different information through relationships with others. Essentially, to make more room at the table. At the same time, it's important to be cognizant of not converting this exercise into a "check the box" activity and forging new relationships for superficial purposes.

Surrounding Yourself with a Trusted Few

It's important to note that the Unaware stage of your journey, and the next stage, Aware, might need to be somewhat private. Think of your budding inclusive leadership skills and mindset as a seedling in a greenhouse. Carefully planted, and still fragile, not ready to brave the elements.

Nurturing and protecting this seedling means seeking or creating a safe place to question, to explore, to awaken, and to begin to gather and test our nascent knowledge and awareness. The learning process is incremental, brick by brick, and counter to so many business and organizational norms that run like clockwork, with their strict timelines and focused and measurable goals. The work of inclusive leadership marches to a different drummer; time must be taken to build a strong foundation. And this pace will look different for each of us.

As we begin to awaken out of the Unaware stage, many of us feel excited and eager to grow faster—to set down those deeper roots more quickly. I recommend curating your "success team" carefully in this early stage so that you don't over-reach beyond your developing capabilities.

Find a trusted few peers, coaches, and mentors from your same identity group and also, more importantly, across other identities. Your tendency, even at this stage, may be to choose the easy path by surrounding yourself with voices who willingly participate in an echo chamber of positive feedback. The support of same-identity people is valuable, but it shouldn't be your only forum in which to grow. I urge you to also reach out to people outside your inner circle, people with different identities and perspectives who are honest and brave enough to point out where you still need to learn and grow.

> *The support of same-identity people is valuable, but it shouldn't be your primary forum in which to grow.*

Those alongside us in these early efforts can support us with honesty and openness, and ideally you will become mutually invested in being each other's booster and champion in seeing one another succeed. You can and should look forward to building and deepening these supportive one-on-one relationships as you travel through the Continuum. Indeed, they are the all-important ingredients that you need not only to stay on top of what others are experiencing, but also to take and adjust your actions.

Remember, people with identities different than your own are not obligated to teach you about how their identities impact them in the world. It can depend on the person, the day they're having, and the context they're in at the moment. A respectful approach takes this into account and doesn't assume that sharing is always easy or simple. It's important to recognize that sharing your experiences, especially as marginalized individuals, is emotional labor and can be exhausting and fatiguing. Many people burn out in the process of being the only ones advocating for change in their organizations and, on top of that, being asked to spend time educating and holding space for others to learn.

As we invite new conversations, it is best to let others set the pace and check in frequently with them. And most importantly, we need to create *mutually beneficial* partnerships and should continually think about what we can bring to them ourselves.

Key Reminders

If you've recognized some of yourself in this chapter, you're hopefully feeling motivated to take a closer look at your potential to become a more inclusive leader. Similarly, if you want to support your colleagues in their journey out of the Unaware stage, this chapter has hopefully provided you with many points of entry to transformational conversations and creative ways to support others in their progress.

Notice if the concepts in the chapter created discomfort; it's helpful to name this in the Unaware stage, and in the next chapter, Aware, to share reflections with your circle of support. You will find you're not alone.

In this chapter, we also dug into the concept of bias and learned to think more critically about how bias shows up in the systems that surround us as well as in ourselves. This is another lens to bring forward with us throughout each stage. Biases will continue to appear; what is most important is that we recognize them and choose to not let them drive our behaviors and actions. An inclusive leader pays close attention to bias, in themselves and others, and develops vigilance over time through daily practice.

As we close this chapter, it is vital that we leave space and grace for ourselves and others in this stage. As we awaken to a new journey, we may grapple with regret, resistance, and self-doubt. The process of moving forward isn't always seamless or smooth; it can be awkward and very imperfect. But every moment is teachable, and every conversation and self-reflection is a part of our growth as we progress.

Inclusive leaders are learners at heart—they have a growth mindset and are curious to learn more about the world around them and to be transformed by it. They believe that there will always be more ahead to process and learn about, and they are unafraid to return to Unaware, again and again, realizing that they don't know what they don't know and have to begin again at the foundation. Even seasoned experts in DEI return to this stage to learn more.

Chapter Discussion Guide

What You Can Do

- Learn more about the experiences of people with different identities. Revisit the history you were taught in school to better understand what may be missing.

- Begin to investigate your biases and examine how they impact your beliefs and how you view the world and the people around you.

- Get out of your echo chamber. Be more intentional about the media you consume, the books you read, the social media channels you follow. Actively seek out perspectives from identities that are different from your own.

Conversation Starters

- Find three different news coverage stories about a recent event and as a group, examine and discuss what biases are informing and impacting these perspectives.

- Ask group members to describe situations in which they have experienced or witnessed bias in society or the workplace. Discuss what could have been done differently in those situations.

- Have group members complete the Inner Circle Inventory and discuss their findings. Strategize what can be done to diversify your perspectives and expand your inner circle.

CHAPTER THREE

Aware

In this stage, you learn more about the concept of privilege and understand better that the playing field is not level for everyone. You educate yourself about your own identities and those of other people and how our identities shape the way we experience the world around us. As you learn more about different lived experiences, you develop empathy and are motivated to contribute to the change effort.

I'm in a conference room with a group of White male senior executives. I'm in my early years as a DEI practitioner, and I have been brought into the company to talk about why DEI matters in response to a PR crisis stemming from claims of harassment and a hostile work environment.

As I start to speak, I notice my palms are sweating. In rooms like this, although I'm not in any physical danger, I still don't feel safe. I'm on high alert before I say a word. I scan the room and confirm that, from what I can observe, I'm the only woman present. It's a familiar feeling, and I am reminded again, in this moment, of the lack of gender diversity in the executive ranks in the business world. I wonder if they've already written me off and how I can overcome this automatic dismissal.

Although I can't be certain, I suspect that I'm also the only person in the room who identifies as a member of the LGBTQ+ community. I'm positive my sexual orientation hasn't crossed their minds because, in many ways, I defy some stereotypes particularly held by certain generations about how someone thus identified *should* look.

As I begin to facilitate the conversation, I'm also calculating: How brave am I feeling? To what extent have I personally experienced the issues we're there to discuss, and should I share these? Does doing so strengthen, weaken, or distract from my argument? Will I have less credibility, in their minds, if I align myself and my personal experiences with people experiencing exclusion and harassment?

I sense my success with this group will be determined by my ability to detach and appear objective. I present my information in a dispassionate, clinical way so that no one can accuse me of positive bias toward certain identities, especially my own. This is necessary because I suspect I am already only holding their attention by a thread, that they are in the room unwillingly, and that they are not interested in addressing any root causes of why we're there in the first place.

After an hour of discussion, I determined that I made the best decision by carefully leaving much of myself out of the conversation. I leave feeling diminished, discouraged, and unsure of how many of those leaders would support and advocate for me as a colleague if we were working together directly. If I worked for that company, I would have serious doubts about my ability—and desire—to stay.

This type of experience is being repeated across workplaces everywhere, every day, and I believe it's a key factor in the difficulties that organizations are facing in retaining talent that reflects the diversity of our world.

Today, I make sure *not* to hide my stories but lead with all of them, in the hopes that by doing so, I can inspire others to do the same. Although I am deeply shaped by difficult experiences as a woman and a member of the LGBTQ+ community, I also am enabled by, and openly talk about, my privileges—I'm White, upper middle class, hold a graduate degree, and have solid financial resources—and the different ways I am learning to leverage them to shift systems around me.

This alignment I have arrived at, however, isn't the norm for most of us who carry underrepresented identities. In working with clients, my company has collected thousands of data points on what disrupts our ability and willingness to bring our full selves to work. Many people report having been either overtly or subtly discriminated against and indicate that they downplay or hide parts of their identities to avoid triggering bias and microaggressions. They sense that it's not worth it to tackle each comment or slight because there is no commitment to change on the part of organizations and their leaders.

We talked about the fatigue of existing in these circumstances on a daily, and sometimes hourly, basis in our last chapter and how it robs talented people and organizations of the best possible performance. When people are actively hiding their identities and unique insights, struggles, and experiences, they aren't able to fully leverage those same things for their success. Not only does this struggle to fit in lead to diminished performance, but it also saps energy that would be better spent working toward helping the organization succeed.

Indeed, brilliance comes from our diversity of identities and perspectives; if we can utilize all of these aspects in our problem solving and strategizing, the result is superior. But this full human potential and creativity can only be unleashed when we feel like we belong, when we have psychological safety and trust with our colleagues, and when our capabilities aren't doubted or downplayed because of biases about us.

> *Our full potential and creativity*
> *can only be unleashed when*
> *we feel like we belong.*

This really is the focus of the Aware stage—to better understand concepts of identity and privilege, how they impact our lived experiences, and what the costs are to individuals and organizations when elements of our identity and experience remain hidden and unexplored.

Hallmarks of the Aware Stage

In the Aware stage, you intentionally set out to learn more about the concept of identity. You learn about the invisible benefits and privileges that certain identities have been afforded and understand better just how unequal the playing field really is. You deepen your understanding of this picture and locate yourself in it. You commit to progress, to personally evolve, and begin to explore what a more proactive role supporting DEI might look like.

In this stage, you learn how your own identities shape your lens of the world and influence your ideas, values, and beliefs, including the judgments and assumptions you form about other people. You also learn more about the identities of other people and understand better how people around you hide parts of their identity to blend into the mainstream and avoid discrimination. You recognize how this both impacts and impedes an individual's success, engagement, and belonging in the workplace.

In the Aware stage, you understand and begin to challenge negative social narratives that exist around certain identity groups. You develop new language and vocabulary that better reflects the current conversation and are able to address others and their experiences in more nuanced and culturally competent ways. You understand how your choice of words can send a powerful inclusive signal to those that you are endeavoring to support.

In this stage, you are confronted with some harsh truths about the many ways people are advantaged and disadvantaged by their identities, and you learn that people are having radically different experiences in society and the workplace. You develop empathy for the lived realities of people from different identity groups and feel motivated to get involved in the change effort.

Developing and Nurturing Empathy

Empathy has no script. There is no right way or wrong way to do it. It's simply listening, holding space, withholding judgment, emotionally connecting, and communicating that incredibly healing message of "You're not alone."

—BRENÉ BROWN

I believe in our capacity to hold many truths and perspectives at the same time and that learning to do so will ignite our empathy and connect us more deeply to others' experiences. Every day, people are managing challenges that deeply affect their lives. Simply being interested in and aware of what other people are going through is an important step toward becoming a more inclusive leader because it demonstrates that you *care*.

Empathy is fundamentally the ability to understand the feelings and experiences of other people, to put yourself into someone else's position and try to imagine how they might be feeling in certain situations, and to recognize why they may act the way they do. We need empathy now more than ever. The world outside companies is chaotic and uncertain, and as we define what it means to be able to bring our full selves to the workplace, it must include the space to be truthful about how the world around us affects us in different ways.

In a long Twitter thread, Nicole Sanchez, a well-respected diversity consultant, described the gulf between our experiences in society and how we are expected to show up fully at work:

> In the past few years, I've been in the position to lead inside companies while major events, all with racism at their core, have unfolded in the news. From the unrelenting videos of police violence against our Black neighbors, to the presence of actual Nazis in our midst, to the Muslim travel ban, to the images of Latinx children in detention camps, leading "business as usual" is not an option.
>
> The reality inside most companies is that the people in the lead are not the ones most deeply affected. I cannot explain the feeling of walking into an office in the midst of these events and being asked with a smile "How was your weekend?" The answer is "My weekend was a racist hellscape, thanks." And the extra painful part is being around people who have the luxury of not paying attention, not fearing for their family's safety, wondering why all the long faces.[1]

This is an example of how the narrowness of what's permitted at work harms so many, and how entrenched it is not to "see" others, especially when you don't share the same lived experiences. The choice that Sanchez is forced to make, between authenticity and bringing her whole self to work or choosing to rise above, if she can, and return to business as usual, feels deeply unfair.

We should never have to choose between our authenticity and bringing our full selves to work.

Diving into Identity

A number of years ago, I participated in my first privilege walk. If you're not familiar with the concept, it's an exercise that forces participants to confront their different identities and the ways in which society privileges some identities over others. The goal is to get people to reflect on their identities, the advantages and disadvantages their identities afford them, and how that locates them in the world.

The exercise is not a perfect one. During it, participants who have less privilege are publicly asked to share their experiences of being marginalized so that people with more privileged identities can learn from the differences. It also often isn't accessible to people with disabilities. That said, it can be a powerful experience.

During the exercise, everyone starts in a horizontal line in the middle of the room. As the facilitator reads aloud a statement or question, participants move either forward or back, depending on their response to the question. Here are a few examples:

MOVE FORWARD IF . . .

One or both of your parents graduated from college.

There were more than 50 books in your house growing up.

You studied the history and culture of your ethnic ancestry in school.

Your family never had to move due to financial hardship.

MOVE BACK IF . . .

You are going to be the first person in your immediate family to graduate from college.

You have ever been the only person of your race/ethnicity in your place of work.

You grew up in an economically disadvantaged or single-parent home.

You have ever skipped a meal because there was not enough money to buy food.

I knew going in to the exercise that it was going to be an awakening and would expose advantages I had by virtue of my identity that others may not have benefited from. But I hadn't anticipated that it would leave me at the front of the room, with very few others around me.

I still remember being overwhelmed by a mix of emotions. Shock, guilt, and shame. It's uncomfortable to face the fact that some people have greater access to resources and opportunities than others. That some of us move through this world with unearned ease while others struggle to simply exist safely and securely because of their identities. This really is the groundwork of understanding identity and how it locates us in the world.

But it's critical to be reminded at this moment that none of us is a monolith. I often think of the Rubik's Cube as a metaphor for the different identities we carry, with each side of the cube representing a different identity. It captures the complex and endless ways our different identities show up and intersect and how some are visible and many others are hidden from view unless the cube is turned.

> *When it comes to identity,*
> *none of us is a monolith.*

For instance, I'm White. This aspect of my identity has enabled me to function more easily in the world, more safely, with more automatic protections. This is one side of my Rubik's Cube. Yet, for most of my adult life, I have identified with and led from a mindset of marginalization as a member of the LGBTQ+ community. This is another side of my cube.

I'm a woman. Another side of the cube. But I'm a White woman, so that's one intersection point with certain identity implications. I may be disadvantaged in the workplace in comparison to men, but I have advantages that women of color don't have. I'm also a queer woman, so that can put me at a disadvantage in certain circumstances compared to a straight woman. This is also an identity that I can hide, where I can "pass."

This concept of intersectionality was originated by Kimberlé Crenshaw.[2] She describes it as being the nexus of multiple stigmatized identities. If you are a woman of color, for example, you have dual stigmatized identities. If you're a queer woman of color, you have triple intersecting stigmatized identities. If you're a queer woman of color with a plus-size body type, you have quadruple stigmatized identities.

The intersections of our identities and how they locate us in the world are myriad and complex. And like a Rubik's Cube, the pieces move around and intersect in countless ways.

As you become more aware of how different identities intersect, you will also realize that many of us carry identities that provide both disadvantages *and* advantages. For the longest time, my privileged and marginalized identities felt like a binary choice, that I couldn't be both privileged in some ways *and* marginalized in others. But the reality is that privilege is not absolute. Privilege can coexist alongside identities that leave us feeling marginalized and disadvantaged.

We all have both visible and invisible aspects of our identity that make us who we are. Some of those are innate dimensions (gender, ethnicity, ability, sexual orientation), and some we acquire throughout our lifetimes (age, parenting, chronic illnesses, mental health issues). Yet many of us spend precious time, energy, and effort hiding or downplaying core elements of our identity to blend in with the dominant culture around us.

This is called "covering" and is also often referred to as masking or code-switching. We do this in anticipation of being negatively stereotyped. We hide parts of our identity to blend in, to avoid conflicts with coworkers. We play smaller, or go quiet, or don't speak up, especially if doing so has fatigued us over time and has actually harmed or impeded our progress.

Covering brings with it an emotional tax and insidiously diminishes our sense of self. Identity covering also impacts productivity and engagement: if a person is preoccupied with stifling or hiding core aspects of their identity, they are not focused on their work.

Covering brings with it an emotional tax and insidiously diminishes our sense of self.

The goal of inclusion is to foster cultures that encourage individuals to bring their full selves to work. This isn't just an end goal in and of itself, but it has everything to do with unleashing potential, engagement, and output. We are able to contribute more of our best creativity when we feel a strong foundation of belonging, of being seen, heard, and valued.

The challenge, then, in Aware is to acknowledge that people around us are struggling to belong, and many are covering important parts of their identity to fit into the dominant organizational culture.

The Tip of the Iceberg

When I work with clients, I often use the metaphor of an iceberg to spark conversations about what it means to cover. Imagine an iceberg floating in water with only certain diversity dimensions evident above the water—for example, physical traits like the color of our skin, our accents or the languages we speak, how we dress, and so on (see Figure 2). These are often what are viewed as "acceptable" per an organization's dominant culture norms. But many other parts of personal identity can remain invisible and unshared below the waterline. Here are just a few:

- I don't talk about my child who has a disability.

- My team doesn't know I have a child who is transitioning.

- I don't attend work events where there is alcohol because I am in AA.

- I don't join colleagues for lunch because I don't want them to know I have an eating disorder.

- My executive team doesn't know I have a spouse in prison.

- My team members don't know that I am in a same-sex relationship.

- No one knows my parents entered the US by crossing the border and that they don't speak English.

- I don't tell people I changed my Chinese name to an American name and took classes to learn an American accent.

- I use vacation days to get treatment for a chronic medical condition.

- I have intense social anxiety and that's why I don't speak up in meetings.

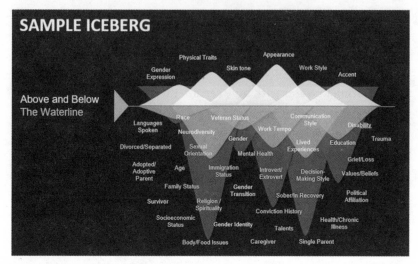

Figure 2. Iceberg

I often work with senior leaders and their teams to help them understand how the iceberg metaphor plays out in people's work experiences. During those discussions, I urge them to reflect on the following questions:

- Which aspects of your identity do you make visible?
- Which aspects of your identity do you keep concealed beneath your waterline?
- What would make you feel comfortable and safe enough to lower your waterline?

In one of the sessions, a leader responded to the challenge to stop covering by coming out as Jewish to his majority Christian management team. In another session, an executive shared that he didn't have a college degree, and that he had hidden that from his coworkers and his own children. Yet another leader shared that he had grown up in an abusive and alcoholic family.

Every one of us is so complex that it makes no sense to assume you know who someone is based on what is evident above their waterline, but people make assumptions about each other nonetheless. Instead, it is immensely helpful to simply be aware that we all have an iceberg where potentially just the tip is showing. Reminding ourselves of this, in each interaction, is the core work in the Aware stage.

For instance, when people meet me or work with me for the first time, they probably assume correctly that they know my race, gender, and generation. But they are likely to misidentify the less observable aspects of who I am, such as my religion, educational background, or sexual orientation.

I also have *passing privilege*, which means I can allow myself to be mistaken for a heterosexual woman and I can choose not to bring up the fact that I have a same-sex spouse. Depending on how comfortable I am in my environment, and what behaviors or attributes are valued in my workplace, I may or may not bring up more of what has shaped my life experiences. If I do, that effectively lowers the waterline of my personal iceberg.

The reality is that many experience the workplace of today as unhealthy, triggering, and toxic. In exploring your own identity in this context, you may discover that you are also covering parts of your identity, and that this is limiting your potential. Of course, you don't need to share all the details of your private life at work, but if you anticipate being negatively stereotyped about a certain aspect of your identity, it takes extra effort to adjust how you show up, and this valuable energy could be diminishing your ability to succeed.

As you work to transform yourself into an inclusive leader, remember that we all know something about diversity through our own experiences and that people around us are covering parts of their identity on a daily basis. In an age in which particularly younger talent isn't going to be persuaded to follow senior leaders based on title alone, it behooves every leader to revisit where they set the waterline on their personal iceberg and to show up more fully and honestly as relatable human beings.

Key Reminders

Curiosity means that we do not take things for granted, that again and again we question even the fundamentals. If you are curious, you will find the puzzles around you. If you are determined, you will solve them.
—ERNŐ RUBIK, THE INVENTOR OF THE RUBIK'S CUBE

Inclusive leaders embody a sense of curiosity and a willingness to dive in and understand some hard truths about the world we live in. They commit to getting involved, to taking action. Without this commitment, change will continue to elude us.

The fundamental question of the Aware stage is "What do I not yet see or understand?" It is one thing not to have known, or been told, information; we might have lacked exposure, and understanding, and maybe curiosity. But it is another thing to admit what you don't know and hold yourself accountable for learning. Throughout this chapter, my hope is that you are beginning to recognize that we are not all starting from the same place, and that many of us are having radically different experiences.

At this stage, you should start thinking seriously about the support you want to give others. As you're learning more, what is making you feel like you want to take action? What has captured your mind and heart? Maybe it's a particular community you belong to. Maybe you're newly committed to overcoming biases you only recently realized you had. Maybe you've realized you want to bring more of your true self to work, both for your own well-being and to role model to others what might be possible for them. Maybe you want to monitor your biases and language more closely and ask for feedback about any microaggressions that are sneaking in. All of these motivations will serve as guides when you enter the Active stage of the Continuum.

Awareness is a powerful stage in the inclusive leader's journey and one that we never really leave; like to home base, we should be returning here often. We cycle back to it as we continue to learn about different people and communities and discover all that we've missed, tuned out, or minimized in our own stories and those of the people around us.

In this stage, what's most important is to keep learning and to keep trying. We can't afford to approach the journey of becoming an inclusive leader with inertia or passivity. Accept that it's going to be challenging and it's going to require you to be uncomfortable. We can't pause our learning until we get it perfect. Change can't wait.

Chapter Discussion Guide

What You Can Do

- Think about your own identities and the way they impact how you show up in the workplace.

- Use the iceberg to understand more about your own identities and those aspects of your identity you chose to keep below the waterline. Challenge yourself to lower your waterline.

- Educate yourself about other identity groups. Examine the assumptions and judgements you make about people from those groups. Understand where these assumptions come from and how biases may influence your perceptions.

Conversation Starters

- Share as a group the ways your organization rewards and/or marginalizes different identities. Examine times people in your organization may have personally benefited from or been disadvantaged because they belong to a certain identity group.

- Discuss as a group the ways in which each individual covers aspects of their identity and why and where they set their waterline.

- Strategize ways the organization and teams can be more inclusive to people from all identity groups.

CHAPTER FOUR

Active

In this stage, you put your learning into action. You take risks in the interests of positive change and embrace a mindset of failing forward. You allow yourself to be vulnerable. You share your story and seek out the stories of other people. You lead and participate in difficult and uncomfortable conversations as learning opportunities. You dive deeper into DEI and get personally involved.

A Chief Diversity Officer (CDO) at a pharmaceutical company relayed a compelling story about her CEO that speaks to how powerful the Active stage can be. A study had been conducted to assess women's advancement in the company, and findings presented to C-suite leaders showed a severe drop off for Black women once they hit senior roles. After a robust dialogue about the findings, she approached the CEO to get his personal take on the data and the discussion. She told me that he shook his head and exclaimed, "I am blown away by this. This cannot be. I had no clue. I'm going to do something about this."

As the meeting turned toward action planning, the CEO posed the idea of spending time with Black women in the organization to better understand their experiences, and get their input on what needed to be done differently. And that's what happened. Despite it being a holiday season, they moved quickly and got the time scheduled for a three-day meeting. The CEO led the effort.

Initially, there was trepidation among the women in the organization who were asked to participate in the session, both about the CEO's motivations and goals for their time together. But after three days that included vulnerable shares, storytelling, and meaningful discussions, all of the participants expressed being transformed by the experience. The women who participated reported they felt valued and supported and that their voices were heard. They were able to raise important issues and instigate changes to practices that perpetuated inequities.

The CEO left the meetings with a much deeper understanding of the impact of workplace culture and bias on this critical segment of employees. In addition, by getting directly involved, he was able to leverage his influence to initiate a series of systems changes that otherwise may have taken years to get off the ground. To this day, he continues to stay involved with the group and has also initiated similar sessions with other employee groups across different identities.

The point is, we all have to start somewhere, even if we don't often know the next steps or have all the answers. This is the danger of the Active stage. I've seen many leaders get stuck here; they want to activate their voice but aren't sure what to say or how to get started. And they want to get it right. Fear that they won't get it right holds many back. Inaction is still action. Staying silent says a lot.

Hallmarks of the Active Stage

In the Active stage, you get off the sidelines. You step into your role in driving change and begin to take some calculated risks. You recognize that interrupting the status quo to make change happen is important work and that your involvement is needed. As your confidence and competence grow, your actions become bolder, more public, more visible.

In this stage, you embrace vulnerability. You share things about yourself in a more open and personal way. By sharing your personal story and experiences, you set an example and cultivate a safe environment in which other people can do the same and share their stories. This is critical to building relationships, respect, and trust across differences.

In the Active stage, you create and hold space for difficult conversations on topics including bias, racism, privilege, and inequity, understanding that these conversations are already happening and that the people around you are impacted in myriad ways by the events unfolding in society and the world around them. By engaging in uncomfortable conversations, you expand your perspectives and mindset and reframe your conventional thinking.

In this stage, you understand the value of DEI in driving business results and in creating an equitable and inclusive workplace. You get involved in DEI programs and initiatives and encourage your team and colleagues to get involved too. You align your business strategy with the DEI strategy and understand that by doing this, you will hold a competitive advantage. If there isn't a DEI program already in place, you advocate for one and get involved in launching it.

*Failure is an inevitable and
essential part of growth.*

In the Active stage, you accept that failure is an inevitable and essential part of growth. You don't let mistakes stall or hold you back, but instead openly welcome the trial and error that comes with growth, and you continue to move forward no matter how imperfectly.

Leaning into Vulnerability

I've learned that people will forget what you said, people will forget what you did, but people will never forget how you made them feel.

—MAYA ANGELOU

Because the road of inclusive leadership is so personal, with the intent to change minds *and hearts*, opening up and sharing more of ourselves, our personal stories, and our struggles and experiences, is crucial. Today's employees want to connect personally with their leaders. They want to know what their leaders think, what they stand for, and what they value. When leaders open up with vulnerability, share their stories and experiences, and tell us about their weaknesses and struggles, they appear more human and approachable. We find them inspiring and easier to connect with, easier to relate to.

I acknowledge that what we're practicing in this stage is counterintuitive to what's been incentivized in so many workplaces. We've traditionally rewarded certainty and decisiveness in leaders. We have not cultivated and measured qualities like humility, empathy, vulnerability, or resilience—characteristics that are critical for today's inclusive leaders.

As leaders, we work hard to present a facade of authority and certainty to the organization, and expressing vulnerability may feel like a weakness or liability. No one is perfect, yet it's become a norm for leaders to appear flawless, like we have all the answers. Not only is it a lot of work to maintain this image, it's also unrealistic and inauthentic.

Vulnerability doesn't detract from a leader's capacity to inspire people. Instead, I think it augments it in powerful and transformative ways. As I work with and coach clients, I regularly challenge leaders in particular to get personal and vulnerable, to share their stories and experiences with their organizations and teams, to show they're a work in progress.

> *Vulnerability doesn't detract from a leader's capacity to inspire people; in fact, I think it augments it in powerful and transformative ways.*

I believe it is especially critical for leaders to do this because thousands of eyes are on them. When a senior leader opens up with authenticity and vulnerability, they can directly impact whether an individual employee, looking upward, sees their story and their background reflected and feels safe enough to share their own identities and stories.

A great example of this is Apple's CEO, Tim Cook, who publicly came out in 2014 after reading a number of letters from kids who were struggling with their identity.[1] It's worth reading the entire letter as an example of a leader sharing their personal story and experiences openly and vulnerably, but here are a few excerpts:

> Being gay has given me a deeper understanding of what it means to be in the minority and provided a window into the challenges that people in other minority groups deal with every day. It's made me more empathetic, which has led to a richer life. It's been tough and uncomfortable at times, but it has given me the confidence to be myself, to follow my own path, and to rise above adversity and bigotry. It's also given me the skin of a rhinoceros, which comes in handy when you're the CEO of Apple . . .

. . . I don't consider myself an activist, but I realize how much I've benefited from the sacrifice of others. So, if hearing that the CEO of Apple is gay can help someone struggling to come to terms with who he or she is, or bring comfort to anyone who feels alone, or inspire people to insist on their equality, then it's worth the trade-off with my own privacy . . . We pave the sunlit path toward justice together, brick by brick. This is my brick.

When leaders are willing to go first and openly and vulnerably share their struggles, their aha moments, even when such moments don't show them in the best light, they create a safe space in which people who have been excluded and marginalized can share their experiences and have their points of view heard and discussed. Feeling seen in this way can shift someone's sense of belonging and unleash creativity, energy, and engagement.

The Power of Storytelling

Many stories matter. Stories have been used to dispossess and to malign. But stories can also be used to empower, and to humanize. Stories can break the dignity of a people. But stories can also repair that broken dignity.

—CHIMAMANDA NGOZI ADICHIE

As humans, we have been telling our stories for thousands of years as a way to share the things we value and care about and to inspire others to value and care about those things too. Stories have the unique ability to shift hearts as well as minds, and often, a story will compel action more than any statistic.

In the workplace, storytelling is a powerful tool to move beyond transactional relationships, to forge deeper connections and engage and interest people in new concepts, ideas, and perspectives. In this spirit, I will share my own story and why I continue to tell it.

Earlier I mentioned that I have been doing DEI work for my entire career, but that's not the entire story. What I didn't mention was that this focus and career path came about only after my childhood dream fell through. I was raised in a musical family and always wanted to pursue a performing career. I loved music and the stage, and in my late twenties got the chance to move to New York City to study vocal performance at a conservatory. It was a dream come true.

But a small rain cloud was approaching from the distance, already foreshadowing the complex future that awaited me. In the midst of my training, I injured my voice and needed vocal surgery. During the recovery period that followed, there were weeks when I wasn't able to speak at all, not even a whisper. When I began to use my voice again, it was a strange, unfamiliar, high-pitched squeak. I would ultimately undergo several more surgeries, as the injury kept recurring. Throughout this time, I was going through a mental and emotional crisis as well as a physical one.

What a lot of people wouldn't know is that there's a huge stigma in the industry about vocal surgery. Who would want to hire me if I wasn't reliable? Just like a professional athlete downplays injuries, I tried to make people believe I was healthy and that everything was normal. I was like that duck—seeming to glide smoothly above the water, but paddling frantically beneath the surface. I had to work through some heartbreaking implications for my career and figure out who I was outside the world of music. I despaired of ever finding a new, equivalent passion.

Although this was one of the most painful periods of my life, it ultimately led me to a career in which I can still parlay my love of the stage and use my voice, but in a different way, as a teacher and advocate. What began as a time of despair ultimately clarified my understanding of what I'm actually here to do and redirected me to where I could be of most value.

I now believe I was always meant to use my voice, just not as a singer. And the voice metaphor continues to deepen. Now I believe I was meant to experience voicelessness, not just literally, but also as a female and LGBTQ+ person in workplace systems that don't see or value people like me. I think I was destined to become a student of how change happens in institutions and to give voice to the voiceless using my platform. And I have come to understand that all of the identities I carry give me access and permission to use my voice and be heard. Quite a revelation—and it all began with what I thought was the end of a dream.

As I crafted my story into my first TEDx talk, I struggled with how to move through painting a picture for my audience of that very dark time in my life into a larger conversation about how that early adversity and disappointment ultimately put me on course for what has become my life's purpose and passion.

I also wrestled with whether I would be judged for how fortunate I've been. To even have the opportunity to study music and work toward a performance career is a privilege available to few. Those same privileges enable me to stand safely on a stage and tell my story, from a distance, as a paid expert and shield me from the very real threats faced by so many in the LGBTQ+ community who pay a steep price when they try to use their voices.

I have come to understand that some of the identities I carry give me access and permission to use my voice and be heard.

I also recognized that if they can't get on that stage, and if I can, then it's up to me to step up. Because I have been given much, I feel compelled to use my voice to create space for other stories—for someone just finding their voice. If my identities can gain me access to the rooms where traditional power exists, I will do everything I can once I'm in those rooms to leverage whatever I have to make sure that progress happens. This is what I can contribute, and in a way, it's what I was destined to contribute.

Sharing my personal story has taken on new meaning for me over many years of retelling it. In processing it again and again, I healed from the devastation of walking away from my operatic dreams. The passage of time has enabled me to see my experiences from a safe distance as the teachers that they are. This is a gift.

The ways audiences have interpreted and taken inspiration from my story over the years has been moving. So many people have come up to me after my speaking events to thank me for sharing my story and have then gone on to tell me their own stories of feeling othered or excluded, of how they have stepped up to adversity and emerged victorious on the other side, and of what they are doing to pull other people along. We build connections and expand perspectives when we can share on a personal and human level like this. It helps us to locate ourselves in the larger human experience.

So now you know my story. I urge you to think about and share your own. But don't get bogged down in the perfect. What we sometimes assume is small and inconsequential about our stories and experiences can often be the one thing that shines a light for others who might be struggling in the dark to follow.

Uncovering Your Story

Over the years I've had the good fortune to host numerous inspirational guests on my podcasts and community forums. So many have shared their personal stories to bring awareness and cultivate empathy for the lived experiences of people with different identities.

Many have overcome structural barriers, discrimination, and personal adversities in their journeys to be their authentic selves.

When I think of the transformative power of storytelling, I think of many stories I could share. The one I'd like to share with you here is that of Joze Piranian.

Joze was born in Lebanon with a severe stutter. As he tells it, he avoided speaking and interacting with people for the first twenty-five years of his life, doing everything he could to cover his stutter. In undergraduate school, he begged his professors to exempt him from presentations and asked for extra homework in lieu of having to participate verbally in the classroom. He was terrified of being judged and saw silence as the only solution to avoid rejection.

When he was twenty-seven, Joze came to realize that covering his stutter was preventing him from forming relationships, from really living. He realized it was up to him to take control of his personal narrative and to find the courage to change his relationship with the fear that was holding him back.

After avoiding speaking publicly for more than two decades, Joze challenged himself to talk to a hundred strangers each week. Over the next four years, he estimates he spoke to tens of thousands of strangers. He describes this exercise as life changing and says he learned through the process that fear and action are not mutually exclusive.

"I love the topic of turning points because it is sometimes based on the romanticized idea of transformation," Joze said. "This idea insinuates that all we need for change is one breakthrough moment when something clicks. I have not found that to be the case. I believe fear and action *can* co-exist. With me, it was what I call millions of micro-moments of bravery when I did what I was afraid of doing again and again and again, until that relationship with fear and discomfort started to transform."

The fodder for stories can come from experiences of marginalization or advantage, from any and all of our lived experiences.

Everyone has a story, and we have all experienced hardships, wins, and losses—experiences that have ultimately made us stronger and more resilient. As Joze Piranian's story so eloquently illustrates, when we open up and share our stories in a vulnerable way, we build empathy and understanding, and at the same time, we inspire and motivate others to uncover and share their own stories.

Today, as an internationally acclaimed speaker, Joze has shared his story with millions of people. By sharing what he has learned by confronting his fears, he creates a way forward for anyone who has let fear get in the way of action.

You too may have heard stories that stick with you. Think about when that has happened and why those particular stories resonated and moved you. You might remember your biases being interrupted by a surprising twist in someone's story that stopped you in your tracks. Maybe you have been personally affected by injustice or unfairness or have witnessed someone you care about disadvantaged in some way. Perhaps there is a story about a loved one, or a valued colleague, whose journey made an impression on you.

I am confident you are sitting on a powerful story yourself. But it can't work its magic if you never tell it. As you begin to uncover your own story, these questions may help you find your voice:

- What was your life like growing up? Did you experience any hardship not shared by some or all of your peers?

- When have you felt the sting of exclusion in your life? What did that feel like? How did you navigate that?

- Can you share a story that reveals a bias you've overcome or helped someone else to overcome?

If you are ready to investigate the structure of your story, I recommend the advice of Erin Weed, founder of Evoso and one of the most talented TEDx speaker coaches I know, about the arc of effective stories, which is Story, Truth, and Universal Truth.[2]

STORY

- What occurred?

- What action was taken?

- How did you change? What did you do differently?

- What changed as a result?

TRUTH

- What did you take from the learning?

- What has been the result over time?

- How do you know it was important or significant?

- What ultimate lesson did you take away?

UNIVERSAL TRUTH

- What can the audience take from your story?

- What can be learned or applied?

- What do you hope for, for others?

Diving into DEI

Up to this point, a great deal of the work in this stage has been at a very personal level; it has required you to self-reflect and learn, to lean into vulnerability, and to open up and share more about yourself. But this stage is also about getting actively involved in the change effort, disrupting the status quo, and applying an equity lens to the systems, policies, and practices that surround you.

The good news is, if your organization has a DEI program, this can be an entry point from which to get started. Whatever your role is, I urge you to learn more about DEI and find ways to get involved. The most successful DEI strategies have commitment from the top, with leaders engaged as full partners and actively involved as spokespersons, sponsors, mentors, council members, and allies. Leadership involvement signals the importance of DEI. It's also a critical factor in securing the budget, human capital, and resources needed to sustain a successful effort.

Without the support and active involvement of leaders, DEI will not become an organizational priority.

There are a number of ways to get involved in and support DEI, some stated here, and they will vary organization by organization. Workplaces are the sum of their parts and each organization is composed of a unique set of systems, demographics, and dynamics.

Get personally involved. I encourage you to prioritize the time needed for meaningful involvement. Don't send a proxy; no one can do this work for you. Your involvement sends the message that DEI is a priority. Leaders' personal involvement creates the followership needed to achieve scalable change and will inspire other people to get involved.

Align commitment with action. You have leverage and influence as a leader. Use it to embed DEI in the business strategy and workplace DNA. Review employee engagement surveys and climate assessments to identify issues and areas for action. Examine recruitment, hiring, and advancement practices for bias and inequities. Reference DEI in decisions. Make the link between DEI and the work you do as an organization and a team.

Leverage DEI in communications. No matter how well developed the DEI strategy is, if it is not communicated effectively by leadership, managers won't take it seriously and employees will tune out. Leaders can play an important role in crafting and delivering the DEI message. Authenticity is crucial: social media platforms and online forums like Glassdoor and LinkedIn have removed the divide between what happens inside a company and external perceptions of the organization. Leaders need to ensure their external messages accurately communicate the organization's internal reality.

Learn more about your organization's ERGs. ERGs can serve as important assets in understanding community needs and experiences in the workplace. They can also play pivotal roles in tapping into new markets and help ensure that products and services developed for those markets are appropriate and culturally relevant. Explore ways you can support the work of ERGs. When leaders are executive sponsors of ERGs they can help guide the efforts, secure resources, and remove obstacles. But it's important not to take over. I have seen organizations set up ERGs and put their leaders in charge of them. Their intention may have been to accelerate the change effort, but in reality, with leaders in the companies in charge, nothing was changing.

Get your own house in order. Set an example. Look closely at your team and reports. Are they representative of the population and communities where you do business? What does that representation look like as you move up in seniority? Who is in your leadership pipeline and succession plan? Question your daily actions. Who are you listening to in meetings? Who are you giving the high-profile assignments to? It's important to ensure that, as leaders, we aren't creating or perpetuating different standards for different groups of employees.

Involve mid-level managers in setting DEI goals. Ensure managers are engaged in the DEI effort and involved in identifying inequities and barriers. Ensure that mid-level managers are equipped with the knowledge, tools, and competencies to lead diverse teams with an equity and inclusion mindset. Accountability at this level is key: managers should be held responsible for their part in developing, implementing, and achieving DEI goals.

Get comfortable talking about difficult and uncomfortable topics. As leaders, we can't continue to avoid conversations around topics like bias, racism, and privilege because they are uncomfortable. These conversations are important, and they are happening already. Dive into these conversations as opportunities to learn more about one another, to create respect and trust across differences. Create a safe space for listening to employees to understand more about how they experience the workplace, what they need, and how you can help meet their needs.

Develop cultural competency. As leaders, we manage people and projects across geographic and cultural contexts while navigating the work styles and expectations of different generations, nationalities, and backgrounds. This is the reality of today's workplace. Culturally competent leaders understand, communicate, and effectively interact with people across cultures. They are aware of their own culturally learned assumptions and biases, and they deliberately cultivate knowledge of different cultural practices and world views.

Become a mentor. Mentorship is a powerful tool for professional development and career advancement, especially for women, people of color, and other marginalized individuals who have historically been left out of the inner workings of an organization. Reflect on how you can leverage your experience, skills, and influence to support and mentor individuals who are underrepresented in the organization. Although we often tend to think of mentorship as a one-way relationship, the reciprocal learning that can happen in mentoring relationships should not be underestimated. Explore what you can learn from your mentees.

Set a personal goal to sponsor someone. Inclusive leaders actively use their power, influence, and networks to sponsor high-potential talent and connect them with stretch assignments, new networks, pay increases, and promotions. I urge you to pay attention to who you sponsor. Does the individual look like you? Do they share the same background and identities? If they do, find someone who doesn't share those characteristics to sponsor as well. Although there are multiple ways to build relationship capital, I have observed that sponsorship creates the single biggest difference in the advancement of underrepresented talent and can have a significant impact on promotion, pay increases, and satisfaction rates.

I encourage you to take the time to learn about the DEI efforts in your organization and how they have progressed over time. Understand what the issues are. Talk to people who are involved in DEI initiatives and learn more about what they are working on and why it is important to them. I do want to extend a word of caution here. Many leaders awaken to the importance of leveling the playing field, of rolling up their sleeves and getting to work, and then jump into DEI efforts and either take over or reinvent already ongoing efforts. In the Active stage, we can think we're doing the best and right thing but still miss the mark.

> *Ask, don't guess how to get involved. Your role is to support and champion DEI efforts, not take them over.*

A powerful example of this was shared with us by an Asian-American employee and member of her company's Asian ERG during the spike in anti-Asian violence in the spring of 2020. The company's leadership had decided to respond to the situation by making a one-time charitable donation to advocacy organizations in the community. The employee shared that if the leadership had first checked in with employees of Asian descent, they would have better understood where support and action were really needed. As it was, Asian employees in the organization were disappointed with the company's response and would have recommended different avenues for community impact. And they sought not just monetary commitment, but leadership solidarity with the community's pain. They wanted to know that their leaders shared their frustration and outrage.

This example highlights the old way of checking the box and the tendency so many leadership teams have of assuming the right remedy without consulting those most impacted. In discussions pertaining to certain groups, it is critical to seek out and listen to their perspectives first and learn where they need the most support, since it is their experience of discrimination and exclusion that you're working to mitigate.

Key Reminders

No magic amount of time is spent at each stage of the Continuum, and this is perhaps never truer than at the Active stage. This stage can feel painstaking and slow as we persist in our efforts but don't yet see the evidence of progress or a positive impact on others and the systems around us. It may be tempting to give in to feelings of powerlessness when you acknowledge the sheer magnitude of effort required to move the needle. But as the stories in this chapter demonstrate, gestures don't need to be grand to make a difference, and every story counts.

Your personal journey toward becoming a more inclusive leader will span many years and involve difficult yet rewarding work. Using your voice and your platform to act effectively, with the desired impact, is a skill that you will develop over time. Taking any action that disrupts the status quo may seem risky. But don't underestimate the power of relatively small commitments enacted by single individuals when it comes to changing systems. When small actions escalate and cascade across an organization, the impact can be transformative.

Gestures don't need to be grand to make a difference.

I remind you to be patient with yourself at this stage. As you start to take action against the status quo, it can be difficult to know what's right, and progress doesn't always mean perfection. But no one is perfect and even the most well-intended among us will make mistakes. In this stage, what's important is to get started, to step out of your comfort zone and begin to take some risks, to stay focused, and to keep moving forward even if the pace of change isn't as flawless or as fast as you hoped it would be.

Chapter Discussion Guide

What You Can Do

- Open yourself up with vulnerability and begin to uncover your personal story. Start to share it with others. Seek out and center the stories of people around you who don't share your identity.

- Learn more about your organization's DEI program and get actively involved in some way. If your organization doesn't have a DEI program, work to get one started.

- Personally commit to becoming a mentor or sponsor to high-potential diverse talent. Don't rule out reverse mentoring and opportunities for your own learning as a mentee of someone with a different set of identities.

Conversation Starters

- Share an example of a story that has inspired you or changed your perspective about something. What was it about this story that was powerful? Encourage people that report to you and on your teams to share their stories.

- As a group, discuss and share the emotions that arise for members when they share their stories. Strategize ways to build psychological safety in the workplace.

- Discuss and identify specific ways your team can embed DEI values in the work it does and how the team can get involved in the organization's larger DEI effort.

CHAPTER FIVE

Advocate

In this stage, you leverage your power and influence to propel change. You draw attention to systemic inequities and get involved in solving them. You work in allyship with others to shift systems and behaviors and take action to disrupt the status quo. You exhibit resilience when you encounter resistance and continue to move forward even when it means breaking away from old norms and groups.

In a 2018 interview with *60 Minutes*, Salesforce CEO, Mark Benioff, described learning about the results of a company-wide pay audit.[1] The results were shocking to him. Like many leaders, he wanted to see his organization and its practices in the best light. But the hard numbers painted a different picture. Benioff admits they found evidence of a gender pay gap everywhere: "It was through the whole company, every department, every division, every geography."

The audit was a wake-up call, and Benioff immediately initiated a wave of sweeping changes to address the disparity. He increased pay for women who were earning less than men for the same work, which cost Salesforce millions. He also instituted a general practice rule: he wouldn't hold a meeting unless 30 percent of the participants were women. This new practice quickly drew attention to all the roles and teams where women were underrepresented.

A second pay audit a year later showed that the gender pay gap had widened again. Salesforce had acquired dozens of smaller firms that brought with them unfair pay practices. Benioff equalized the salary differences, spending millions again.[2] But ongoing annual assessments found that wage gaps reappeared without constant scrutiny. With each audit, Salesforce identified new factors to consider and fixed the points of failure that were discovered. Benioff acknowledged, "We're going to have to do this continuously. This is a constant cadence."

Other leaders and organizations take note of actions such as this. It can be powerful role-modeling to see and hear respected leaders choosing to change, to become more equitable, and to do the work of dismantling and rebuilding inequitable systems in a public way. Benioff was very transparent about the pay disparities when he learned about them, and he openly shared the steps the company took to address them. Transparency is an important leadership trait. When what has been neglected, hidden, or protected is made visible, public accountability is created.

Progress plays out this way. Sometimes it starts with big public actions like the ones Benioff took around pay equity. Sometimes it's with smaller, more private actions, like giving more space for different voices in meetings and letting someone else have the floor. Sometimes it starts just by asking some seemingly simple questions: Why is it like this? Is it fair to everyone? How did this happen? What are we going to do to change it?

When what has been
neglected, hidden, or protected
is made visible, public
accountability is created.

Hallmarks of the Advocate Stage

In the Advocate stage, you lean into a new type of leadership. You treat people as equals no matter what their roles are and make room at the table for different insights and perspectives. You recognize that people who are affected by marginalization and inequities are in the best position to help you understand the issues and what is really going on in the organization. You understand that shared decision-making leads to better decisions and more equitable outcomes.

In this stage, you are deeply committed to the work of allyship. You understand the inequities and exclusion different identity groups experience, and you align yourself in solidarity with them. You leverage your power, influence, resources, and social capital to help speed their impact. You recognize that being an ally is not a label you give yourself, but rather one that you earn through your words and your actions. You take responsibility for your impact and you own it when you miss the mark.

As an advocate, you question underlying policies, practices, and assumptions, even if you are an "insider" who benefits from them. You think the status quo is unacceptable and are unafraid to challenge norms and assumptions or risk ostracization from your peers. You model the way for others to stand up to discrimination and inequity. You build your own capacity to take high-stakes risks that contribute to meaningful action.

In this stage, you build resilience. You don't let failure or mistakes derail you; you keep moving forward. You recognize people will question your motives and go out of their way to point out your flaws, but you persevere, even in the face of resistance. You continually push yourself to be and do better.

Developing Resilience to Weather the Storm

Pushing to address root causes of inequitable systems and biased practices does not come without risk. And the risk level increases as you become more public about your actions and advocacy in this stage. As you bring attention to problematic systems and behaviors, you create accountability and begin a conversation, which is a good thing. But you may also risk ostracization from your in-group because you are telling the truth and breaking a code that protects them.

You can pay a price for stepping outside of and challenging and disrupting protected systems. Even when you're trying to help people and evoke positive change, some people will have a negative reaction. There has always been a constant push and pull between those people that are willing to disrupt the status quo and those who are unreceptive to change.

As you step into your role as an advocate and ally, people may accuse you of having biases for particular groups, question your motivations, or go out of their way to point out your mistakes. If your motives are questioned or your methods are criticized, listen, consider, and adjust if necessary, then persevere. It's important to anticipate pushback so you aren't caught off guard by people who aren't as far along on their journey to becoming inclusive leaders.

The true measure of leadership is not how an individual performs during the good times, but the fortitude they display during times of uncertainty and their willingness to take a stand—especially when the stakes are high—and to persevere in spite of resistance.

Whether they like it or not, organizations and their leaders are expected to take a stand on important societal issues. Often this pressure comes from employees and customers, and sometimes, the general public.

If your motives are questioned or your methods are criticized, listen, consider, and adjust if necessary, then persevere.

Today's corporate leaders are increasingly using their influence and reach to take highly visible political and social positions on behalf of their employees and customers. I remember when Dick's Sporting Goods stopped selling assault weapons at its stores following the Marjory Stoneman Douglas High School shooting. The company's CEO, Ed Stack, found himself in the headlines and the subject of some significant backlash.

In an open letter, Stack explained the decision to pull the weapons off shelves: "We support and respect the Second Amendment, and we recognize and appreciate that the vast majority of gun owners in this country are responsible, law-abiding citizens. But we have to help solve the problem that's in front of us. Gun violence is an epidemic that's taking the lives of too many people, including the brightest hope for the future of America—our kids."[3]

The company had the option to send the weapons that were removed from its stores back to manufacturers for a refund. Another possibility would be to liquidate the merchandise through discounts. But Stack believed if Dick's sold off the guns or sent them back to the manufacturers, they would end up back on the streets. Instead, the company destroyed $5 million worth of assault rifles.

Dick's received praise from gun-control advocates for the move. But social media reaction from detractors was fierce and provoked consumer boycotts of the company. NRA and its supporters publicly bashed the CEO's decision. A number of firearms manufacturers ended their relationship with the company. As key players in the gun industry turned against the company, the company adjusted its growth plan. But Dick's said customer traffic ultimately improved despite the controversy. The company's tough—and very public—stance on the topic also paved the way for other major retailers, including Walmart, to impose stiffer gun sales regulations.

Whatever side of gun control you're on, stories like these demonstrate that with every challenge comes a tremendous opportunity to propel important societal change. It takes resilience to keep moving forward in the face of resistance or when it feels like the amount of change that is called for is insurmountable. But leaders in the Advocate stage commit for the long term. They are marathoners, not sprinters.

Leaning into Allyship

You do not have to be me in order for us to fight alongside each other. I do not have to be you to recognize that our wars are the same. What we must do is commit ourselves to some future that can include each other and to work towards that future with the particular strengths of our own individual identities.

—AUDRE LORDE

At a rally in Harlem following the church shooting in Charleston, South Carolina, Features writer Rose Hackman captured the comments of Feminista Jones, a thirty-six-year-old social worker and writer, who shouted into a bullhorn, "It's not about being on the outside and saying 'Yes, I support you!' It's about 'Not only do I support you, but I am here with you. I am rolling up my sleeves. What do I need to do?'"[4] I think this example describes what we need from allies. It's being prepared and at-the-ready to provide support and take direction. This is the energy that's needed at the Advocate stage.

At the same time, this does not mean you should make yourself the center of attention by taking over completely. As a White leader and aspiring ally, I am always cognizant of not replicating the *White savior complex*, a term coined by Teju Cole, a Harvard professor.[5] White saviorism is when White people, in an effort to ally themselves with any marginalized community, are guided by the impulse to save or rescue that community. Many well-intentioned White people actually end up inadvertently robbing marginalized communities of their agency by implying that without White intervention or support, marginalized communities could not help themselves and there would be no progress. Although White saviors are passionate about doing the right thing, their actions often involve very little input from the very communities they're attempting to advocate for and support.

Allyship is not self-defined. Our work and our efforts as allies must be recognized as valuable by the people we seek to align ourselves with. We are only an ally when someone in an affected community calls us an ally. And sometimes the best allyship means knowing when to step back to ensure those most affected are included, centered, and prioritized. In my own allyship journey, I am always mindful of a popular rallying cry of the disability rights movement: "Nothing about us without us." Before you move into action, it's important that you spend the time to really listen to those community members you hope to support and that you think deeply about the impact of your intentions and actions before you jump in.

It's critical here to understand the difference between *intent* and *impact* when it comes to allyship. Essentially, the impact of an action, behavior, or statement is more important than the intent behind it. If our actions unwittingly offend, hurt, or further marginalize someone else, there is usually an opportunity present for further learning. But often, instead of focusing on the impact of our actions or words, we jump to explaining our intentions or stubbornly defending ourselves. Being allies means holding ourselves accountable when we make mistakes, apologizing, and committing to improvement.

> *We are only an ally when those within the community we intend to support call us an ally.*

I also wanted to point out that allyship happens on a very individual and personal level, but in an organization, if allyship is cultivated and nurtured, it can also become embedded in the organizational culture and DNA.

At Accenture, the company's Disability ERG launched a Mental Health Allies program to create mental health awareness and provide support and resources to employees in a safe space.[6] The program engages volunteer employees from across the company who are committed to supporting mental health awareness and education and who are available to listen and provide support. A special Mental Health Ally lanyard identifies them as someone who is informed and approachable for anyone who wants to talk.

Although Accenture's mental health allies are not trained psychologists, psychiatrists, or therapists, they are educated and trained in mental health topics, and often they have experienced a mental health condition themselves. In 2018, the program included more than 6,000 members, engaged more than 1,200 allies, and had chapters in the US and across 27 Accenture offices worldwide. It is when we are able to stand in solidarity and support one another that important issues get addressed and real change happens throughout an organization.

It's important to remember that allyship can spring from any one of our many identities. It's not just a binary relationship or only the province of those of us with more privileged identities. Men can be allies to women. White people can be allies to people of color, cisgender people can be allies to members of the LGBTQ+ community, members of the LBGTQ+ community can be allies to veterans, veterans can be allies to communities of color, and so on.

What motivates us to align ourselves with other identity groups can be workplace driven, like the Accenture example I used earlier, or it can be very personally motivated. Richard Jeanneret, a senior executive at EY, was inspired to become an advocate and ally to the LGBTQ+ community by the experiences and actions of his son, Henry, who came out as transgender in his senior year in high school.[7] After he transitioned, Henry wasn't allowed to use the boys' locker room or play on boys' sports at his school. He experienced exclusion in many different ways. But the experiences also fueled Henry's motivation to become an advocate for the community.

Henry's experiences and activism deeply affected Jeanneret. He in turn became an advocate for the community and worked to help other senior executives at EY learn more and better understand how amending the civil rights legislation to protect LGBTQ+ professionals in the workforce was good for business. When Jeanneret had the company's support, he leveraged the power of the firm to help get his message heard on a national level, including on Capitol Hill.[8]

Although all messengers need to be prepared with arguments, language, and a heavy dose of resilience, our identities will impact whether and how we are heard. Those of us with privileged identities may get pushback, but we will usually get less of it. Ultimately, Jeanneret's message spread so widely (at least in part) because of his identity as a cisgender White male and his professional status as a senior leader.

Sustainable and meaningful change requires multiple messengers, from all levels and identities. The inclusive leader instinctively knows when to step forward when the message needs to come from them. But at the same time, they understand the need to include a more complete representation of voices to achieve more meaningful, equitable, and informed outcomes.

Allyship in Action

Allyship needs to be authentic. Superficial words, slogans, or one-off commitments to allyship are increasingly being called out and criticized as performative when they aren't followed by meaningful action.

A good example of this is all the companies who posted a black square on social media to signal solidarity with the Black community following the murder of George Floyd. While the gesture may have been well-intended, it often wasn't backed up with any real action.[9] Although numerous companies did make a range of public commitments to support Black communities and Black employees in 2020, studies that were done a year later to assess the status and outcomes of those efforts found few of these initiatives had come to fruition.[10] It can be damaging to signal good intentions, and then not follow through with meaningful action.

There are many ways to show up effectively as an ally and advocate. I have made some aspects of allyship part of my daily habits and practices. For example, when I am invited to participate as a guest on a panel, before I accept, I make sure that there is diversity among the invited speakers. If there is not, I decline to participate, explain why, and offer to recommend another identity and voice to fill my spot.

It can be damaging to signal good intentions, and then not follow through with meaningful action.

Given that I identify as cisgender, I make a point to share my pronouns as often as I can and ensure I know how others identify and use their desired pronouns. In my virtual keynote presentations, I encourage participants to add their pronouns to their participant profile name on Zoom. I see them typing in "she/her/hers," "he/him/his," "they/them/theirs," and for some, it's likely their first time doing so. Some don't participate in the practice, but I know a seed has been planted.

My company hosts three forums (the Will to Change podcast, Community Calls, and Advocacy in Action) that are open and free for anyone to attend. Our goal for the sessions is to educate, increase awareness, and create space for all voices. Guests represent a diverse range of backgrounds and identities and share their stories and experiences. Topics covered include gender parity, addressing bias in recruitment and hiring, developing cultures of belonging, tapping into untapped talent pools, mentoring and sponsorship strategies, increasing representation at senior levels, and many others. We have delivered hundreds of these conversations and brought awareness to tens of thousands of participants. This is another way of standing in solidarity and allyship with marginalized communities.

As I hope these examples demonstrate for you, you can step into the role of an ally in many ways, both big and small. Here are a few guidelines to get you started on your own journey of becoming an ally and advocate:

Acknowledge your privilege. Be cognizant of your identities and how they are viewed, permitted, rewarded, or penalized in the systems and structures around you. Pick your head up to look more objectively and critically at what surrounds you, what supports you, and how your experience might be—and likely is—specific to you and your place in the world and the workplace.

Listen more and speak less. Hold back on your opinions and ideologies, and resist the urge to "save" the people you are standing in solidarity with. Examine how you may be complicit in perpetuating stereotypes, biases, and discrimination just by existing in the workplace. Do your own research on the inequities and oppressions people of other identities and backgrounds experience, and don't expect marginalized communities to educate you.

Be an upstander, not a bystander. Single microaggressions often go unnoticed because they are small moments. But when they are repeated and pervasive, their impact can add up and take a toll on those who are experiencing them. Call out microaggressions, inequities, and discrimination when you see them. Amplify and reinforce upstander behaviors in others. Silence sends an unintended message, leaving employees to interpret it in their own way. Inaction is still action.

Build your resilience. Embrace the emotions that come out of the process of allyship. Understand that you will feel uncomfortable, challenged, and hurt. Unpack why you are feeling the way you are and use this information to propel your allyship journey. Be honest and accountable with your mistakes, and recognize that being called out for making a mistake is an opportunity to be a better person, to learn, to grow, and to do things differently.

Do not expect awards or special recognition for confronting issues that people have to live with every day. If you do receive recognition for your work as an ally, redirect that attention back to the groups you are supporting and use the opportunity to increase awareness around the issues they face.

Challenging Systems and Structures

Real change starts with recognizing that we are part of the systems we seek to change.

—PETER SENGE ET AL.

Standing in solidarity with people who may not benefit from the dominant systems means looking critically at those same systems, even if you are an insider who benefits from them. This is hard work. It can be painstakingly slow, with many dead ends and a limited fanbase. It can mean breaking with groups we are a part of, and there is, of course, risk in this. But leading is not without risk, by definition.

Inequity is deeply entrenched throughout society and the workplace, and the reality is, the systems around us benefit some and disadvantage many others. In our work with clients, we have found bias and inequities embedded throughout workplace systems and policies including recruitment and hiring, promotions, professional development, succession planning, performance reviews, compensation, and many more. Everywhere we look in organizations, there is opportunity to address biased behaviors and inequitable systems. We can literally start almost anywhere in our analyses.

Many processes that companies follow perpetuate bias because they've never been critically examined under a systems lens. When we begin to question and disrupt systems, many of us will learn more deeply just how inequitable and discriminatory they are, and sometimes we recognize painfully how our own unexplored biases and behaviors may have contributed to or perpetuated the problem. Part of the resilience we need to build at this stage is the ability to humbly acknowledge this, be accountable for it, but at the same time, not let it hamper our progress.

It's also critical to recognize that changing systems and behaviors isn't a journey you take alone. Change doesn't happen in a vacuum.

I have worked with leaders who hoard their power and think they have all the answers. They get stuck in their own point of view and aren't willing to engage with views that are different from their own. They don't recognize the limitations of their identity and experience lenses and how harmful it is not to understand others' experiences. Sometimes these individuals reject or resist change efforts because they haven't been included in the discussion and the proposed solutions haven't accounted for their needs. Regardless of the reason, leaders in this mode are most interested in protecting the status quo and perceive any change as a threat.

But I have also worked with leaders who intentionally make room at the table for different perspectives even when they don't align with their own. These leaders know the difference between when their voice and leadership are needed and when others need to be heard and empowered to lead. This type of leader spends time meeting with people at all levels to better understand what needs to be changed. They rely on the input they gather to make decisions, and they check back often to make sure those decisions are resulting in more equitable outcomes. The most skilled among them strategize constantly about how to build community, marshal commitment, and engage those in power in the effort. This is, in effect, the inclusive leader.

We can begin changing behaviors and systems by asking and reflecting on some fundamental questions. Here are a few to get you started:

- What do I notice in my organization, at the systems level, that I can challenge? What are others noticing?

- Where do I feel especially safe challenging processes, people, and biases at work? Do I have special access or influence that other people do not? How could I make the most of those advantages?

- What type of risk am I willing to take in order to advocate for change? What types of risks can I afford to take?

- Who has my back and is in my support system should I need them? Who will be my key partners?

- How can I be more public in how I advocate for change? How will I sustain my efforts?

It may seem like systems managed by people are basically unfixable because of the entrenched reality of bias. Far from being powerless, advocates at every level of a company learn how and when to ask powerful questions and to challenge norms as well as move conversations toward more public commitments to change.

Ultimately, being an advocate is an opportunity to move beyond the superficial approach to something deeper that gets to the heart of the issue. I like to think of the Advocate mindset as asserting: I *will* identify systemic inequities in whichever organization I'm in, and if I can use my power and privilege to make lasting, sustainable change, then I'm going to do that.

Key Reminders

Change takes time. Leaders love short cuts and quick fixes. So much business jargon proves how obsessed we can be with key takeaways and next steps and how we view progress as linear, with a destination and a completion date. But change doesn't always work like that. If you're actively working to drive change, you have to be patient. Showing up as an ally and advocate requires constant self-reflection, resiliency, and the humility to keep learning from our mistakes. What's most important is to keep trying, to keep moving forward.

If you've been working hard to make change happen and haven't received a lot of personal feedback, don't be afraid to check in with your team members and ask how they think you've been doing. It's imperative for every inclusive leader to take that time to get feedback, calibrate, and ready themselves for a bigger role in the conversation, and perhaps in more public conversations, which they can then step into as advocates. That practice is the training, if you like, before the big match.

We can't expect to be good at this right out of the gate. We are going to have to apologize when our impact doesn't match our intent. And that is par for the course. I think a lot about failing forward, the agility and flexibility of getting feedback, adjusting, and trying again. It's about getting a little better each time. This is about practice, taking it from an intellectual exercise to an embodied way of being. Inclusive leadership isn't a goal or a destination, it's the embracing of a journey, where skills are built, day by day, experience by experience.

A final word about courage and resilience in the Advocate stage. As we question things as they are, we are faced with the fact that in doing so, what we benefit from personally and professionally may shift. Our power may feel different and begin to come from a different source. Some experience this as destabilizing, or even threatening. Our learning, then, is to see beyond this to the other side of what's possible when we work in solidarity with others. The possibilities are limitless.

Chapter Discussion Guide

What You Can Do

- Identify what groups and communities you want to stand in solidarity with. Learn more from them about how you can get involved as an ally and advocate.

- Think about the power and influence you have as an individual in the organization and how you can meaningfully leverage it to propel positive change in your organization.

- Model upstander behavior. Call out inequities, microaggressions, and discrimination. Amplify and reinforce upstander behaviors when you see them.

Conversation Starters

- As a group, discuss the inequitable processes and systems that may exist in your organization and on your team.

- Identify strategies and opportunities for encouraging and supporting allyship in your organization.

- As a group, examine and identify how bias and discrimination show up in the organization's values, systems, and practices. Create awareness about what is discovered and propose strategies for addressing the inequities the group uncovers.

CHAPTER SIX

Staying Committed
to the Journey

If there is no struggle, there is no progress.

—FREDERICK DOUGLASS

If you only remember one thing from this book, remember that to be an inclusive leader, you need to *do something*. Change is about action. And if you aren't taking action, your silence is a passive acceptance of the status quo, which further perpetuates the problem. Good intentions are not enough. Our legacies as leaders will be measured by our impact, and this impact is defined not by us, but by others—those we aim to support and stand alongside. It is crucial that we move decisively, and adjust constantly, to ensure the impact we envision is becoming a reality.

> *If you only remember one thing from this book, remember that to be an inclusive leader, you need to do something.*

Assuming Responsibility for Your Role

Assuming responsibility sounds like a simple thing, but social psychology tells us otherwise. As human beings, we are hardwired to believe that someone else will step in and do the hard work so that we don't have to. In fact, the more people who witness an injustice, the less likely people are to step forward and help. This is called the *diffusion of responsibility*.[1] The term became mainstream after the 1964 rape and murder of Kitty Genovese in New York City, when a reported thirty-eight people heard or saw her attack, but no one called the police or tried to intervene. Apparently, everyone assumed someone else would help. When news of this tragedy spread, the world was baffled that so many people could have stepped in to save Genovese's life but didn't.

Understanding why this crime wasn't stopped is important for us to comprehend why all kinds of ongoing harm are allowed to continue. We falsely believe that our need to intervene decreases as the number of witnesses increases. In a world that's more connected than ever before, the number of witnesses is exponential, and we can hide and just observe ever more frequently. When we hear about injustices through the media, social media, or through the grapevine at work, or when we witness them directly, it's easy to assume it's someone else's fight and to look the other way. We get stuck in "What would I do or say?"—and end up doing or saying nothing.

Taking Action

When I think about how diffusion of responsibility continues in the workplace, particularly when it comes to DEI and challenging systemic inequities, I pay attention to three kinds of people. Two are well-understood: those individuals who are content to maintain the status quo and don't see a need for change and those who challenge exclusionary behaviors and systemic inequities. The latter are typically the people who are marginalized by the same colleagues and systems they are challenging. These are the same kinds of brave actors we readily identify in all social movements everywhere in the world, whether against racism and gender-based discrimination or in ethnic struggles between majorities and minorities.

But there has always been a third regularly overlooked group: we don't see its members showing up in the struggle for equity. These are the bystanders, the people who remain on the sidelines by choice, fear, or ignorance but who have so much capacity to make a contribution. Many tell themselves that the fight isn't their fight, or if it is, that they lack the invitation or the tools to intervene and make any kind of positive difference. This inaction has held back our evolutionary progress, but this group has the most potential to become upstanders who shift outcomes for others, and in themselves.

> *I believe we can all be transformative and be transformed in the process.*

If you find yourself in the first group, I encourage you to consider what's possible if you stop spending energy protecting and begin exploring your power and influence and expanding what's possible for yourself and others if you join in the transformation of the status quo. I urge you to stand up as an advocate and ally in solidarity with groups who are marginalized by systemic oppression and open yourself to a total perspective shift. If you find yourself in the second group, I acknowledge how exhausting and taxing this work can be. I stand in solidarity with you.

If you find yourself in the third group, as a bystander waiting for permission or feeling frozen in place, I hope this book helps you find your voice and your role in the change effort and that you develop your upstander capabilities. There is much work ahead, and it will be accomplished more quickly and more effectively with each one of us contributing what we can, from our unique vantage point in the world. These capabilities are available to all of us, ready and waiting to be activated.

Key Reminders

This book has likely given you a new perspective when it comes to all kinds of issues in the workplace—and outside of it. You might feel like an advocate on behalf of some people but like you're still moving out of unawareness when it comes to others. That's to be expected. Remember that the Inclusive Leader Continuum is not a linear journey, and you must be patient with your progress. You may travel forward and backward in your level of understanding and advocacy, but the important thing is that you are committed to the journey.

As someone who has made inclusion my life's work, I still regularly expose myself to new ideas, new voices, and new strategies for working toward equality. I travel through the Continuum regularly, which keeps me humble and even more aware of how much work is to be done. When I encounter people who aren't as far along on their journey, I do my best to reach back through the Continuum and try to pull them from unawareness to awareness all the way to advocacy.

This effort sometimes feels frustratingly slow. It's hard not to feel fatigued and wonder if I'm making a difference. On my own journey, it's been essential for me to find and harness my motivation so I don't give up when times are hard. I seek the company and community of others traveling the Continuum and plug in my battery with them for a while, sharing stories, missteps, successes, and learnings. Doing this reminds me that I'm not alone in my efforts and enables me to reflect on what I could improve or do differently. Sometimes this work has no clear answers, and we are writing the script for the first time.

And sometimes, my battery gets a fast and full charge with one fleeting moment—one comment or one heartfelt "thank you." I've come to expect that even in sessions where there is a lack of diversity and a lot of deflections fill the room, someone always sneaks by me at the end of a session and quietly says, "Thanks for being here today. I'm looking at this in a different way now, and I understand why it's important." That person may not have had the courage to speak up much in the meeting, but something shifted for them. And I believe they will begin to create a ripple effect in their own ecosystem as that shift of understanding begins to take root and grow to fruition.

As you work to figure out what keeps *you* motivated, I urge you to stay connected with the meaning behind supporting inclusion. I deeply believe that getting work done together has always been about feeling included. Human potential is unleashed when we feel like we belong. This goes beyond what we functionally know and do—our job tasks and deliverables. Yes, we want to shine and be acknowledged for our accomplishments, but we also want to trust that others will see—and seek out—our uniqueness; that they'll view it as a positive and not be biased against our difference. We also want to feel our commonality with others—a sense of community, of sharing experiences, of feeling less alone.

The qualities that make us different are far from irrelevant; they are core to who we are, why we do what we do, and how we get our energy. We do better work when we feel like the different aspects of our identity are celebrated and we belong. Difference, when met with inclusive behaviors, enables higher-quality problem solving through *creative abrasion*, where ideas are productively challenged, avoiding the dangers of groupthink. This is the magic behind great organizations; employees who feel valued create more valuable organizations that are able to innovate, to pivot, to calibrate, to anticipate and respond, and to care.

*The qualities that make us
different are far from irrelevant;
they are core to who we are,
why we do what we do, and
how we get our energy.*

As a leader, you can do a seemingly endless number of things to
support a more inclusive environment where everyone can thrive.
Even when you feel like you're powerless—just one person in a huge
organization—or you have little decision-making power, or you're up
against deeply entrenched biases, you can still make a difference with
your own actions. The desire to feel welcomed, valued, respected, and
heard on a daily basis is universal. When you fill that need for your
coworkers, and awaken that need in yourself, so much is possible.

Throughout my many years of working with professionals to
create more inclusive and equitable workplaces, I've noticed that the
most beloved leaders consider themselves students. They humble
themselves and keep stepping into new conversations, spaces, and
skill sets. They practice what's uncomfortable, proactively gaining
exposure and new networks so that they can learn and grow. And
rather than believing they have nothing to contribute when it comes
to diversity, equity, and inclusion, they recognize that they are part
of the solution. Although they might not have all the answers on how
to make an impact, they empower themselves to keep learning.

I wrote this book to help individuals better understand how they
can make small changes that create a resounding impact, no matter
what their title or industry or how far along the Continuum they
find themselves. But personal courage and transparency must be met
halfway at the organizational level in the form of colleagues, managers, and leaders. It's a two-way street.

The environment we create can activate a new level of authenticity in the workplace. But if we take a leap of faith in terms of bringing our full selves to the workplace, the net must appear to catch us. That net is organizational and leader readiness; as workplaces are inhabited by more and more courageous and authentic leaders, is the system preparing and evolving to receive them and ensuring that they can thrive? We need each other, more than ever, to capture the promise of inclusion and make it a reality. As the fight for inclusion gains even more momentum, I believe we'll reach a critical mass when things will start to change exponentially. The wheels are already in motion and, if we continue to focus on unleashing the power of difference and building unity, I believe we're in for amazing changes.

> *What role can we play in evolving our environment so that people of all identities and experiences can thrive?*

As this book comes to an end, remember that inclusion is a daily practice. And as with any habit, change takes practice. I look forward to witnessing the fruits of your efforts to create workplaces where everyone has opportunities to thrive.

Notes

Chapter Two

1. Eyder Peralta, "Microsoft CEO Backtracks on Suggestion That Women Shouldn't Ask for Raises," *NPR*, October 9, 2014, *https://www.npr.org /sections/thetwo-way/2014/10/09/354964666/microsoft-ceo-backtracks -on-suggestion-that-women-shouldnt-ask-for-raises*.

2. Jennifer Liu, "These Are the Best CEOs for Diversity, According to Employee Reviews," *CNBC*, July 20, 2020, *https://www.cnbc.com/2020 /07/20/the-best-ceos-for-diversity-according-to-comparably-employee -reviews.html*.

3. Jennifer Brown, "Sports, Stereotypes and Sexual Orientation: Lessons from a Gay Ex-NFL Player," Jennifer Brown, Speaker, Author, Humanist [podcast], July 13, 2018, *https://jenniferbrownspeaks.com/2018 /07/13/sports-stereotypes-and-sexual-orientation-lessons-from-a-gay -ex-nfl-player/*.

4. Dana Wilkie, "How DE&I Evolved in the C-Suite," *SHRM*, accessed March 21, 2022, *https://www.shrm.org/executive/resources/articles /Pages/evolving-executive-dei-diversity-c-suite.aspx*.

5. Justin Wolfers, "Fewer Women Run Big Companies Than Men Named John," *The New York Times*, March 2, 2015, *https://www.nytimes .com/2015/03/03/upshot/fewer-women-run-big-companies-than -men-named-john.html*.

6. Harvard Implicit Bias Test, *Project Implicit*, 2011, *https://implicit.harvard .edu/implicit/takeatest.html*.

7. Amy Waninger, *Networking Beyond Bias: Making Diversity a Competitive Advantage for Your Career* (Lead At Any Level, 2018).

Chapter Three

1. Nicole Sanchez, "In the Past Few Years, I've Been in a Position to Lead Inside Companies . . .," Twitter, June 19, 2018, *https://twitter.com /nmsanchez/status/1009260622884757505.*

2. Kimberlé Crenshaw, "Demarginalizing the Intersection of Race and Sex: A Black Feminist Critique of Antidiscrimination Doctrine, Feminist Theory and Antiracist Politics," *University of Chicago Legal Forum* issue 1, article 8 (1989): 139–167.

Chapter Four

1. Tim Cook, "Tim Cook Speaks Up," *Bloomberg*, October 30, 2014, *https://www.bloomberg.com/news/articles/2014-10-30/tim-cook -speaks-up.*

2. Erin Weed, "Dare to Be Authentic," TedTalk, October 17, 2017, *https://www.youtube.com/watch?v=bQQfFguY1vo.*

Chapter Five

1. Cindy Robbins, "2017 Salesforce Equal Pay Assessment Update," *Salesforce* [The 360 blog], April 4, 2017, *https://www.salesforce.com /blog/2017/04/salesforce-equal-pay-assessment-update.html?d =70130000000tP4G%20.*

2. Marcel Schwantes, "The CEO of Salesforce Found Out His Female Employees Were Paid Less Than Men. His Response Is a Priceless Leadership Lesson," *Inc.*, June 26, 2018, *https://www.inc.com/marcel -schwantes/the-ceo-of-salesforce-found-out-female-employees-are-paid -less-than-men-his-response-is-a-priceless-leadership-lesson.html.*

3. Associated Press, "Here's What Dick's Sporting Goods CEO Ed Stack Wrote about His Company's Actions," *USA Today*, February 28, 2018, *https://www.usatoday.com/story/money/retail/2018/02/28/heres -what-dicks-sporting-goods-ceo-ed-stack-wrote-his-companys-actions /381452002/*.

4. Harlem rally after Church shooting, Rose Hackman, "'We Need Co-Conspirators, Not Allies': How White Americans Can Fight Racism," *Guardian,* June 26, 2015, *https://www.theguardian.com/world/2015 /jun/26/how-white-americans-can-fight-racism*.

5. Teju Cole, "The White Savior Industrial Complex," *The Atlantic*, March 21, 2012, *https://www.theatlantic.com/international/archive/2012/03 /the-white-savior-industrial-complex/254843/*.

6. Barbara Harvey, "What Companies Can Do to Help Employees Address Mental Health Issues," *Harvard Business Review*, December 18, 2018, *https://hbr.org/2018/12/what-companies-can-do-to-help-employees -address-mental-health-issues*.

7. Richard and Henry Jeanneret, "Out Leadership and PwC present 'Out to Succeed,'" Out Leadership, YouTube, June 22, 2018, *https:// www.youtube.com/watch?v=TyaTwVsNL2w*.

8. Out Leadership, "PwC and Out Leadership Launch Unique New Study of LGBT+ Emerging Business Leaders," *Cision: PR Newswire*, April 30, 2018, *https://www.prnewswire.com/news-releases/pwc-and-out -leadership-launch-unique-new-study-of-lgbt-emerging-business-leaders -300638618.html*.

9. Karen Attiah, "#BlackOutTuesday Was a Case Study in How Performative Solidarity Goes Awry," *Washington Post*, June 3, 2020, *https://www .washingtonpost.com/opinions/blackouttuesday-was-a-case-study-in-how -performative-solidarity-goes-awry/2020/06/03/0b9c42b8-a5e4-11ea -b473-04905b1af82b_story.html*.

10. "From Pledge to Progress: Corporate America One Year after George Floyd's Death," *Seramount*, 2021, *https://seramount.com/wp-content /uploads/2021/08/From-Pledge-to-Progress-Corporate-America-One-Year -After-George-Floyds-Death.pdf*.

Chapter Six

1. Alex Lickerman, "The Diffusion of Responsibility," *Psychology Today*, June 14, 2010, *https://www.psychologytoday.com/us/blog/happiness -in-world/201006/the-diffusion-responsibility*.

Resources for Inclusive Leaders

- For helpful resources and an assessment to help you determine where you are on your inclusive leader journey, please visit *inclusiveleaderthebook.com*.

- This book is also available as an audio book and as an ebook. For bulk orders, please send an email to *info@jenniferbrownconsulting.com*.

- To listen to Jennifer's acclaimed podcast, search for *The Will to Change* on Apple Podcasts, Google Play, Spotify, Stitcher Radio, or your favorite podcast streaming service.

- To find out more about Jennifer and hire her to speak at your organization, visit *jenniferbrownspeaks.com* or email *info@jenniferbrownconsulting.com*.

- To learn more about Jennifer Brown Consulting's services and training programs and to download thought leadership papers for inclusive leaders, please visit *jenniferbrownconsulting.com*.

Acknowledgments

I often share that the work of inclusion and belonging in organizations found me—and not the other way around—that I have had the amazing fortune to learn from and be in community over the last twenty years with some of the bravest, most strategic voices that exist in the conversation about building a new, more equitable world. I am deeply grateful for all the guests who have so generously shared their stories and wisdom on our podcasts, community calls, and webinars, and for the audiences who have sought us out for learning, inspiration, and comfort.

In response to forces none of us could have anticipated over the last few years, our community has fiercely coalesced around the urgency for a different kind of leadership, and for organizations who commit to putting inclusion and equity at their core. As a result, the Inclusive Leader Continuum model in this book in particular has found an enthusiastic audience who utilizes it as an accessible framework to open new doors and conversations and to build trust and common language so the work can begin. I believe this second edition will continue in this tradition and expand the conversation even further. Whether you're a long-time supporter of my books and our work or are just joining our family now, I express my thanks and welcome you to the journey.

I couldn't do this work alone as a solo practitioner and am so grateful for the amazing team that works alongside me through thick and thin. Thank you to my team at Jennifer Brown Consulting (JBC) for the learning, collaboration, and commitment they consistently exhibit. This talented, passionate group of people brings their skills and knowledge to our client work every day. Our reach and ability to have lasting impact depends on them.

And within this team, a small and intrepid group agreed to tackle the writing of a second edition with me—a new experience for all of us. For me as an author, nothing compares to the gratification of having writing partners who care just as deeply as I do about making our writing as powerful as it can be. Thinking the second edition would contain about 10 percent updated content, we happily dug in—and quickly realized we wanted to keep the core model and rewrite the rest (and I've been apologizing since then)! But in all seriousness, as we all put our shoulders to the wheel, we became convinced that the book that had become such a go-to resource for so many could be even more powerful, transformative, vivid, and practical. I hope you agree that we accomplished that.

Two people in particular have been my steady partners in the writing and updating of this new edition. First, to Karen Dahms, a hearty and heartfelt thank you and gratitude for your expansive and deep well of best practices and powerful stories and your ability to capture just the right concepts and wording to ensure our readers stay engaged and feel equipped to lead change in the world. Your passion and commitment shine through the text. And Varshini Balaji, thank you for contributing your expertise and imbuing this book with the clarity and directness that it needed. You kept all the plates spinning amidst challenging timelines, always with positivity, wisdom, and insight.

In the last several years, I've delivered hundreds of presentations, which is only possible because I am exquisitely supported by a world-class speaking team who is passionate about our message and ensures that each talk or project we undertake is as impactful and seamless as possible. First, to Veronica Pirillo, I am so blessed to have you as my invaluable partner as we evolve our message and as we thoughtfully guide our clients on their learning journey. They are impacted as much by working with you as by my message. Holly Kalyn, thank you for the excellent day-to-day support you so consistently provide. You never fail to keep us all connected and coordinated and me as prepared as possible for the inevitable twists and turns in our path. To Parker Jesse, thank you for your beautiful work on our special projects that I am eager to share with the world. And to my colleagues Rob Beaven, Katie Livornese, and Adrienne Lawrence who keep our best-in-class consulting engine and marketing efforts running, I know that we are delivering excellence every single day because you are each amazing at what you do. I am proud beyond words of what we accomplish.

We are again grateful to our editor Steve Piersanti at Berrett-Koehler for his guidance on this edition, as well as to the whole BK community for their support.

And lastly, to my family, thank you for the unconditional support and the love you've shown me for so many years. It has been a rare blessing to have two sisters whose company I happily seek. To my parents in particular, I appreciate every day the means I was fortunate enough to be born into, which has meant that I have been as prepared and equipped as I can be to communicate my message far and wide, and to get up on stage after stage, fearlessly and with joy.

Index

Goldsmith, Marshall, 6
Grace Hopper Conference (2014),
29–30

H
Harvard Implicit Bias Test,
39–40
Hispanic community, 21
humility, 32–33

I
iceberg metaphor, 57–60
identities
covering, 56
and intersectionality, 54–55
and privilege walks, 53–54
unshared, 57–59
see also privileges; workplace
identity
impact vs. intent, 89–90, 98, 101
Inclusive Leader Assessment, 12
Inclusive Leader Continuum,
9–12, 104
see also Active stage;
Advocate stage; Aware stage;
Unaware stage
inclusive leaders
DEI practices for, 74–78
journey to becoming, 10–13,
25–26, 98
qualities and skills, 6–8, 45,
60, 106
inclusiveness, 105
inequity
COVID-19 pandemic, 21–22
recognizing, 17–18
and systemic failures, 3
workplace, 1–2, 95
Inner Circle Inventory, 40–42

intent
following through on, 92
vs. impact, 89–90, 98, 101
intersectionality, 54–55
intervention and responsibility,
102

J
Jeanneret, Richard and Henry, 91
Jones, Feminista, 88–89

K
King, Martin Luther, Jr. (MLK)
on change, 15
on justice, 18

L
leaders
choosing vulnerability, 66–68
in DEI engagement, 16–18,
19–20, 78–79, 96, 102–104
Fortune 500 CEOs, 37
see also inclusive leaders;
specific people
LGBTQ+ community, 4, 91
Lorde, Audre, on allyship, 88

M
marginalized communities
respectful approaches toward,
34–35, 43–44, 94
responsibilities toward, 19
and White saviorism, 89
and workplace equity, 9
Mental Health Allies program
(Accenture), 90
mentorship, 77–78
microaggressions, 36, 94
Microsoft, 30–31

About the Author

JENNIFER BROWN (she/her/hers) is an award-winning entrepreneur, speaker, diversity and inclusion consultant, and bestselling author. As the founder and CEO of Jennifer Brown Consulting (JBC), a twenty-year-old certified woman- and LGBTQ+-owned industry-leading DEI consulting firm, Jennifer and her team are best known for their process of designing workplace DEI strategies and educational programming that have been implemented by some of the biggest companies and nonprofit organizations in the US and globally, including FedEx, Hearst, American Red Cross, Under Armor, Major League Baseball, the National Basketball Association, Toyota, Wells Fargo, and many more.

Jennifer envisions inclusive organizations where *all* of us can thrive. As someone who has experienced both the advantages of privilege and the sting of stigma, Jennifer is boldly redefining what it means to truly belong—in the workplace, in our families, and in our communities—and she openly shares her powerful and unforgettable true story with audiences to help us challenge our assumptions—about ourselves, about leaders, and others—and take inspired action today for a more inclusive tomorrow.

Jennifer is a sought-after keynote speaker for executive leadership on the topic of leading inclusively in uncertain times and has presented at many top conferences and events such as the International Diversity Forum, the Global D&I Summit, the Forum on Workplace Inclusion, the NGLCC International Business & Leadership

Conference, the Out & Equal Workplace Summit, Emerging Women, SHE Summit, Responsive Conference, the Better Man Conference, INBOUND, Alt Summit, South by Southwest (SXSW), PBWC (Professional BusinessWomen of California), the Pennsylvania Conference for Women and Texas Conference for Women, and HR Transform.

She has been featured in media such as the *New York Times*, the *Wall Street Journal*, *Harvard Business Review*, *Adweek*, *Bloomberg Businessweek*, *Forbes*, *Inc.*, CBS, and many more. In addition, she sits on the Influencer Advisory Board for cultural intelligence consultancy sparks & honey, as well as L'Oreal's Global Diversity, Equity & Inclusion Advisory Board.

Her thought leadership accolades include Top Small Business Female Executive in 2019 (*DataBird Business Journal*), peopleHum's Power List of the Top 200 Thought Leaders to Follow in 2021, a Top 50 D&I and Gender Equality Influencer by Onalytica, one of Engagedly's Top HR Influencers, and an Inspirational Diversity & Inclusion Leader of the Year by d&i Leaders Global Benchmarking Survey 2021.

Jennifer is the bestselling author of three books, the first being *Inclusion: Diversity, The New Workplace and The Will to Change*. The first edition of this book, *How to Be an Inclusive Leader: Your Role in Creating Cultures of Belonging Where Everyone Can Thrive*, was named one of Catalyst's 5 Must-Read Books on Workplace Diversity, Equity, and Inclusion in 2021, a shortlist winner of the OWL Award, winner of the 2019 Nautilus Book Awards' Business & Leadership category, and a top SABA 2020 Book Awards Audience Vote. The book and its Inclusive Leader Continuum have found a large and enthusiastic audience as a tool for mindset and behavior change in a wide array of organizational systems, from corporate leadership to academia to trade associations. Jennifer also recently coauthored a groundbreaking book on diversity, equity, and inclusion in society with thought leader and fellow bestselling author, Rohit Bhargava. The book,

Beyond Diversity: 12 Non-Obvious Ways to Build a More Inclusive World, was announced as a *Wall Street Journal* bestseller and listed in *Inc.*'s 22 Books to Read (or Reread) in 2022. It also won Gold in the prestigious Axiom Business Book Awards for 2022.

Her popular podcast, *The Will to Change*, appeared on Feedspot's Top 15 Diversity and Inclusion Podcasts You Must Follow in 2020, and as the host of over 200 episodes, Jennifer interviews leading CEOs, bestselling authors, and entrepreneurs about how we must continue to courageously evolve to ensure greater equity in today's and tomorrow's workplaces.

For information on JBC's consulting and training services, please visit us at *www.jenniferbrownconsulting.com*.

To learn more about Jennifer's speaking services, please visit us at *www.jenniferbrownspeaks.com*.

About Jennifer Brown Consulting

Jennifer Brown Consulting (JBC) believes in unleashing the power of human potential, embracing diversity, and helping people—and organizations—thrive. The company is on a mission to set a new tone for business, and the world, and to create a more inclusive reality for generations to come by helping organizations create the type of workplace where people no longer feel pressure to downplay aspects of their identity in order to survive; instead, they begin to feel free to bring their authentic selves to work and motivated to contribute in a way that fuels bottom-line growth.

As a leading certified woman- and LGBT-owned strategic DEI consulting firm, JBC understands how important it is to empower leaders to drive positive organizational change and the future of work in today's rapidly changing business landscape. JBC partners with HR, talent management, diversity and inclusion, and business leadership teams on change management efforts relating to human capital everywhere from North America to Southeast Asia.

Whether JBC is building interactive workshops on bias, assessing gaps in employee experience, setting up diversity councils, or leveraging its proprietary ERG Progression Model to transform resource groups into trusted business partners, everything is customized to resolve each client's unique challenges.

Past clients include Walmart, Starbucks, Toyota Financial Services, Microsoft, the City of New York, T-Mobile, and many others, from the Fortune 1000 to government agencies and nonprofits. JBC has worked with clients at all stages of their diversity and inclusion journey by meeting its clients where they are and guiding them all the way through. Get in touch today to assess your readiness for change with a free consultation: visit *jenniferbrownconsulting.com* or email *info@jenniferbrownconsulting.com* and mention this book.

Berrett–Koehler
Publishers

Berrett-Koehler is an independent publisher dedicated to an ambitious mission: *Connecting people and ideas to create a world that works for all.*

Our publications span many formats, including print, digital, audio, and video. We also offer online resources, training, and gatherings. And we will continue expanding our products and services to advance our mission.

We believe that the solutions to the world's problems will come from all of us, working at all levels: in our society, in our organizations, and in our own lives. Our publications and resources offer pathways to creating a more just, equitable, and sustainable society. They help people make their organizations more humane, democratic, diverse, and effective (and we don't think there's any contradiction there). And they guide people in creating positive change in their own lives and aligning their personal practices with their aspirations for a better world.

And we strive to practice what we preach through what we call "The BK Way." At the core of this approach is *stewardship,* a deep sense of responsibility to administer the company for the benefit of all of our stakeholder groups, including authors, customers, employees, investors, service providers, sales partners, and the communities and environment around us. Everything we do is built around stewardship and our other core values of *quality, partnership, inclusion,* and *sustainability.*

This is why Berrett-Koehler is the first book publishing company to be both a B Corporation (a rigorous certification) and a benefit corporation (a for-profit legal status), which together require us to adhere to the highest standards for corporate, social, and environmental performance. And it is why we have instituted many pioneering practices (which you can learn about at www.bkconnection.com), including the Berrett-Koehler Constitution, the Bill of Rights and Responsibilities for BK Authors, and our unique Author Days.

We are grateful to our readers, authors, and other friends who are supporting our mission. We ask you to share with us examples of how BK publications and resources are making a difference in your lives, organizations, and communities at www.bkconnection.com/impact.

Dear reader,

Thank you for picking up this book and welcome to the worldwide BK community! You're joining a special group of people who have come together to create positive change in their lives, organizations, and communities.

What's BK all about?

Our mission is to connect people and ideas to create a world that works for all.

Why? Our communities, organizations, and lives get bogged down by old paradigms of self-interest, exclusion, hierarchy, and privilege. But we believe that can change. That's why we seek the leading experts on these challenges—and share their actionable ideas with you.

A welcome gift

To help you get started, we'd like to offer you a **free copy** of one of our bestselling ebooks:

www.bkconnection.com/welcome

When you claim your **free ebook**, you'll also be subscribed to our blog.

Our freshest insights

Access the best new tools and ideas for leaders at all levels on our blog at ideas.bkconnection.com.

Sincerely,

Your friends at Berrett-Koehler

Certified

Corporation